Emanuel Swedenborg

The Doctrine of Faith of Life for the New Jerusalem,

from the Commandments of the Decalogue

Emanuel Swedenborg

The Doctrine of Faith of Life for the New Jerusalem,
from the Commandments of the Decalogue

ISBN/EAN: 9783337182625

Printed in Europe, USA, Canada, Australia, Japan

Cover: Foto ©Lupo / pixelio.de

More available books at **www.hansebooks.com**

THE

DOCTRINE OF LIFE

FOR THE

NEW JERUSALEM,

FROM THE

COMMANDMENTS OF THE DECALOGUE.

BY EMANUEL SWEDENBORG.

BEING A TRANSLATION OF HIS WORK ENTITLED

"DOCTRINA VITÆ pro Nova Hierosolyma ex Præceptis Decalogi.
Amstelodami, 1763."

LONDON:

PUBLISHED BY THE SWEDENBORG SOCIETY,
(INSTITUTED 1810.)
36 BLOOMSBURY STREET, OXFORD STREET, W.C.

1864.

CONTENTS.

THE DOCTRINE OF LIFE

FOR THE

NEW JERUSALEM.

I. THAT ALL RELIGION HAS RELATION TO LIFE, AND THAT THE LIFE OF RELIGION IS TO DO GOOD.

1. EVERY man who has any religion knows and acknowledges, that he who lives well will be saved, and that he who lives wickedly will be condemned; for he knows and acknowledges, that he who lives well thinks well, not only about God, but also concerning his neighbour; but not so he who lives wickedly. The life of man is his love; and what a man loves, he not only does with pleasure, but also thinks with pleasure. The reason, therefore, why it is said that the life of religion is to do good, is, because doing good makes one with thinking good; and unless they make one with man, they do not belong to his life. But these things are to be shewn in what follows.

2. That religion has relation to life, and that the life of religion is to do good, every one who reads the Word sees, and while he is reading, acknowledges. These things are contained in the Word:—*Whosoever shall loosen the least of these commandments, and shall teach men so, he shall be called least in the kingdom of the heavens; but whosoever shall DO and TEACH them, the same shall be called great in the kingdom of the heavens. For I say unto you, that except your RIGHTEOUSNESS shall exceed the righteousness of the Scribes and Pharisees, ye shall not enter into the kingdom of the heavens* (Matt. v. 19, 20). "*Every tree* THAT BRINGETH NOT FORTH GOOD FRUIT *is hewn down, and cast into the fire; wherefore by their* FRUITS *ye shall know them"* (Matt. vii. 19, 20). "*Not every one that saith unto me, Lord, Lord, shall enter into the kingdom of the heavens, but he* THAT DOETH THE WILL *of my Father who is in the heavens"* (Matt. vii. 21). *Many will say to me in that day, Lord, Lord, have we not prophesied in thy name?—and in thy name done many wonderful works? But then I will confess to them, I never knew*

you; depart from me, YE THAT WORK INIQUITY (Matt. vii. 22, 23). *Every one that heareth my words* AND DOETH THEM, *I will liken him unto a prudent man who built his house upon a rock;—but every one that heareth my words* AND DOETH THEM NOT, *shall be likened unto a foolish man who built his house upon the sand* (Matt. vii. 24, 26). Jesus said, *A sower went forth to sow;—some seed fell on the hard way;—some fell upon stony places;—some fell among thorns;—and some on good ground. That which was sowed on good ground is he who heareth the Word and considereth it; who thence* BEARETH FRUIT, AND BRINGETH FORTH, *some a hundredfold, some sixty, and some thirty.* When Jesus said these words, he cried out saying, *He that hath ears to hear, let him hear* (Matt. xiii. 3—9, 23). *" The Son of Man shall come in the glory of his Father;—and then shall he render to every man* ACCORDING TO HIS WORKS" (Matt. xvi. 27). *" The kingdom of God shall be taken from you, and given* TO A NATION BRINGING FORTH THE FRUITS THEREOF" (Matt. xxi. 43). *When the Son of Man shall come in his glory,—then shall he sit upon the throne of his glory;—and he shall say to the sheep on the right hand, Come, ye blessed of my Father, possess as an inheritance the kingdom prepared for you from the foundation of the world;* FOR I WAS HUNGRY, AND YE GAVE ME MEAT; I WAS THIRSTY, AND YE GAVE ME DRINK; I WAS A STRANGER, AND YE TOOK ME IN; I WAS NAKED, AND YE CLOTHED ME; I WAS SICK, AND YE VISITED ME; I WAS IN PRISON, AND YE CAME UNTO ME. *Then shall the righteous answer, When saw we thee so? And the King shall answer and say unto them, Verily, I say unto you, Inasmuch as ye have done it unto one of the least of these my brethren, ye have done it unto me. And the King shall speak in like manner to the goats on the left; and because they have not done such things, he shall say, Depart from me, ye cursed, into everlasting fire, prepared for the devil and his angels* (Matt. xxv. 31—46). "BRING FORTH FRUITS WORTHY OF REPENTANCE;—*and now also the axe is laid to the root of the trees; every tree therefore,* WHICH BRINGETH NOT FORTH GOOD FRUIT, *is hewn down and cast into the fire"* (Luke iii. 8, 9). Jesus said, *Why call me, Lord, Lord,* AND DO NOT THE THINGS WHICH I SAY? *Every one that cometh to me, and heareth my sayings,* AND DOETH THEM, *is like unto a man who built a house, and laid the foundation upon a rock;—but he that heareth* AND DOETH NOT, *is like unto a man who built a house on the ground, without a foundation* (Luke vi. 46—49). Jesus said, *My mother and my brethren are these, who hear the word of God* AND DO IT (Luke viii. 21). *Then shall ye begin to stand and knock at the door, saying, Lord, open unto us;—but he answering shall say unto you, I know you not whence ye are:*—DEPART FROM ME, ALL YE WORKERS OF INIQUITY (Luke xiii. 25, 27). *This is the judgment, that light is come into the world, but men loved darkness rather than light, because*

THEIR DEEDS WERE EVIL; *every one that doeth evil hateth the light,—lest* HIS DEEDS *should be reproved. But he who doeth truth cometh to the light, that his deeds may be made manifest, because* THEY ARE WROUGHT IN GOD (John iii. 19—21). *And they* THAT HAVE DONE GOOD *shall come forth to the resurrection of life* (John v. 29). *"We know that God heareth not sinners, but if any man worship God,* AND DO HIS WILL, *him he heareth"* (John ix. 31). *"If ye know these things,* HAPPY ARE YE IF YE DO THEM" (John xiii. 17). *He that hath my commandments* AND DOETH THEM, *he it is that loveth me,—and I will love him, and will manifest myself to him;—and I will come to him, and make my abode with him. He that loveth me not,* KEEPETH NOT MY WORDS (John xiv. 21, 23, 24). Jesus said, *I am the true vine, and my Father is the husbandman; every branch in me that* BEARETH NOT FRUIT, *he taketh away; but every branch* THAT BEARETH FRUIT, *he purgeth it,* THAT IT MAY BRING FORTH MORE FRUIT (John xv. 1, 2). *"Herein is my Father glorified,* THAT YE BEAR MUCH FRUIT, *and be made my disciples"* (John xv. 8). *Ye are my friends,* IF YE DO WHATSOEVER I COMMAND YOU.—*I have chosen you,*—THAT YE SHOULD BRING FORTH FRUIT, AND THAT YOUR FRUIT SHOULD REMAIN (John xv. 14, 16). The Lord said to John, *Unto the angel of the church of Ephesus write,* I KNOW THY WORKS:—*I have against thee, that thou hast left thy former* CHARITY:—*repent, and* DO THE FORMER WORKS; *or else I will remove thy candlestick out of his place* (Rev. ii. 1, 2, 4, 5). *To the angel of the church of Smyrna write,* I KNOW THY WORKS (Rev. ii. 8, 9). *To the angel of the church in Pergamos write,* I KNOW THY WORKS;—REPENT (Rev. ii. 12, 13, 16). *To the angel of the church in Thyatira write,* I KNOW THY WORKS AND CHARITY—*and* THY LATTER WORKS *are more than the first* (Rev. ii. 18, 19). *To the angel of the church in Sardis write,* I KNOW THY WORKS; *that thou hast a name that thou livest, but art dead;*—I HAVE NOT FOUND THY WORKS PERFECT BEFORE GOD;—REPENT (Rev. iii. 1—3). *" To the angel of the church in Philadelphia write,*—I KNOW THY WORKS" (Rev. iii. 7, 8). *To the angel of the church of the Laodiceans write,*—I KNOW THY WORKS;—REPENT (Rev. iii. 14, 15, 19). *"I heard a voice from heaven, saying, Write, blessed are the dead who die in the Lord from henceforth: yea, saith the Spirit, that they may rest from their labours;* THEIR WORKS DO FOLLOW WITH THEM" (Rev. xiv. 13). *A book was opened, which is of life; and the dead were judged according to those things which were written in the book,* EVERY ONE ACCORDING TO THEIR WORKS (Rev. xx. 12). *"Behold, I come quickly, and my reward is with me;* TO GIVE TO EVERY MAN ACCORDING AS HIS WORK SHALL BE" (Rev. xxii. 12, 13). Likewise in the Old Testament it is written: *"Recompense them* ACCORDING TO THEIR WORK, AND ACCORDING TO THE DOING OF THEIR HANDS" (Jer. xxv. 14). *Jehovah, whose eyes are open upon all the ways of men,* TO GIVE TO EVERY ONE ACCORDING TO HIS WAYS, AND ACCORDING TO THE FRUIT OF HIS WORKS (Jer. xxxii. 19). *"I will visit him* ACCORDING TO HIS WAYS, *and recompense to him* HIS WORKS" (Hosea iv. 9). *Jehovah hath dwelt with us* ACCORDING TO OUR WAYS, ACCORDING TO OUR WORKS (Zech. i. 6). And in many places it is enjoined that men should do the statutes, commandments, and laws; as in the following: *"Ye shall observe my statutes, and my judgments,* WHICH IF A MAN DO, HE SHALL LIVE BY THEM" (Levit. xviii. 5). *" Ye shall observe all my statutes and my judgments,* THAT YE MAY DO THEM" (Levit. xix. 37; xx. 8; xxii. 31). Blessings are pronounced, if they do the commandments, and curses if they do them not (Levit. xxvi. 4—46). The children of Israel were commanded to make to themselves a fringe on the borders of their garments, that they might remember all the precepts of Jehovah TO DO THEM (Numb. xv. 38, 39; Deut. xxii. 12). And in a thousand other places the same doctrine is taught. That works are what make the man of the church, and that according to them he is saved, the Lord also teaches in the parables,—the greater part of which imply, that they who do good are accepted, and they who do evil are rejected; as in the parable concerning the husbandmen in the vineyard (Matt. xxi. 33—44); concerning the fig-tree which did not yield fruit (Luke xiii. 6, 9); concerning the talents and minas given to trade with (Matt. xxv. 14—31; Luke xix. 13—25); concerning the Samaritan who bound up the wounds of him that fell among thieves (Luke x. 30—37); concerning the rich man and Lazarus (Luke xvi. 19—31); and concerning the ten virgins (Matt. xxv. 1—12.)

3. That every one who has any religion, knows and acknowledges that he who lives well will be saved, and that he who lives wickedly will be condemned, is on account of the conjunction of heaven with the man who knows from the Word that there is a God, that there is a heaven and a hell, and that there is a life after death. From thence there is this common perception. Wherefore, in the doctrine of the Athanasian Creed, concerning the Trinity, which is universally received in Christendom, this also is universally received, which is said in the conclusion of it, viz. :—" Jesus Christ, who suffered for our salvation, ascended into heaven, and sitteth at the right hand of the Father Almighty, whence he shall come to judge the quick and the dead; *and then they that have done good shall enter into life eternal, and they that have done evil into everlasting fire.*"

4. Yet there are many in the Christian churches who teach that faith alone is saving, and not any good of life, or good work; they add also, that evil of life or evil work does not condemn those who are justified by faith alone, because they are in God and in grace. But it is remarkable that although they teach such doctrines, yet they acknowledge,—from a

common perception derived from heaven,—that they who live well are saved, and they who lived wickedly are condemned. That they still acknowledge this, is evident from the Exhortation which is read in the churches, before the people who come to the Holy Supper, as well in England, as in Germany, Sweden, and Denmark. It is well known that in these kingdoms there are those who teach the doctrine of faith alone. The Exhortation which is read in England before the people who come to the sacrament of the Supper, is this:—

5. "The way and means to be received as worthy partakers of that Holy Table, is, first, to examine your lives and conversations by the rule of God's commandments, and wherein soever ye shall perceive yourselves to have offended, either by will, word, or deed, there to bewail your own sinfulness, and to confess yourselves to Almighty God, with full purpose of amendment of life; and if ye shall perceive your offences to be such as are not only against God, but also against your neighbours, then ye shall reconcile yourselves unto them, being ready to make restitution and satisfaction, according to the uttermost of your powers, for all injuries and wrongs done by you to any other, and being likewise ready to forgive others that have offended you, as ye would have forgiveness of your offences at God's hand; for otherwise the receiving of the Holy Communion doth nothing else but increase your damnation. Therefore if any of you be a blasphemer of God, a hinderer or slanderer of His Word, an adulterer, or be in malice or envy, or in any other grievous crime, repent you of your sins, or else come not to that Holy Table; lest after the taking of that Holy Sacrament the devil enter into you, as he entered into Judas, and fill you full of all iniquities, and bring you to destruction, both of body and soul."

* 7. It was granted me to ask some of the English clergy who professed and preached the doctrine of faith alone (which was done in the spiritual world), whether, while they were reading this exhortation in their churches,—in which faith is not mentioned,—they believed that it is true, that if any do evil, and do not repent, the devil will enter into them, as he entered into Judas, and bring them to destruction both of body and soul? They replied, that in the state in which they were while reading the exhortation, they knew and thought no otherwise than that these things were religion itself; but that when they began to compose and perfect their sermons or discourses they thought differently, because they thought of faith as the only means of salvation, and of the good of life as a moral accessory to it, for the public good. But still they were convinced, that they had also a general perception that he who

* Paragraph n. 6 in the original, is merely a translation of the above Exhortation into Latin, and is therefore omitted.

lives well is saved, and he who lives wickedly is condemned; and that they had this perception when they were not under the influence of their own *proprium* [selfhood].

8. The reason why all religion has relation to life, is, because after death every one is his own life; for the life remains the same which he had in the world, and is not changed;—for an evil life cannot be converted into a good life, nor a good life into an evil life, because they are opposites, and conversion into an opposite is extinction. It is because they are opposites that a good life is called life and an evil life is called death. Hence it is that religion has relation to life, and that the life of religion is to do good. That man after death is such as his life has been in the world, may be seen in the work on HEAVEN AND HELL, n. 470—484.

II. THAT NO ONE CAN DO GOOD, WHICH IS REALLY GOOD, FROM HIMSELF.

9. The reason why to this day scarcely any one knows whether the good which he does be from himself or from God is, because the church has separated faith from charity, and good is of charity. A man gives to the poor, assists the needy, endows temples and hospitals, promotes the welfare of the church, of his country, and his fellow-citizens, diligently attends public worship, devoutly listens and prays, reads the Word and books of piety, and thinks about salvation,—and does not know whether he does these things from himself or from God. He may do the same things from God, or he may do them from himself. If he does them from God, they are good; if from himself, they are not good. Yea, there are like good works done from self, which obviously are evil,—as are hypocritical good works which are deceptive and fraudulent.

10. Good works done from God, and from self, may be compared with gold. Gold which is gold from its inmost, and is called fine gold, is good gold; gold alloyed with silver is also gold, but it is good according to the alloy; and gold alloyed with copper is less good. But gold artificially made, and only resembling gold in color, is not good; for the substance of gold is not in it. There is also gilding; as gilded silver, copper, iron, tin, and lead, as well as gilded wood, and gilded stone,—which likewise may superficially appear as gold; but since they are not gold, they are estimated either according to the workmanship, or according to the value of the gilded material, or according to the worth of the gold that may be scraped off. These things differ in excellence from gold itself as the clothes differ from the man. It is possible even that rotten wood, and dross, yea, and dung, may be overlaid with gold. This is gold which may be compared with pharisaical good.

11. Man has known from science whether gold is in sub-

stance good, whether it is alloyed or counterfeit, or whether it is overlaid; but he has not known from science whether the good that he does is in itself good. This only he has known: that good from God is good, and that good from man is not good. And since it concerns his salvation to know whether the good that he does be from God, or whether it be not from God, therefore it is to be revealed. But before it is revealed, something shall be said concerning the different kinds of good.

12. There are civil good, moral good, and spiritual good. Civil good is that which a man does in conformity with civil law: by this good, and according to it, he is a citizen in the natural world. Moral good is that which a man does in conformity with the law of reason: by this good, and according to it, he is a man. Spiritual good is that which a man does in conformity with spiritual law: and by this good, and according to it, he is a citizen in the spiritual world. These goods follow in this order; spiritual good is the highest, or first, moral good is the mediate, and civil good is the lowest, or last.

13. The man who is in spiritual good is a moral man, and also a civil man; but the man who is not in spiritual good, appears as if he were a moral and civil man, and yet is not. The reason why the man who is in spiritual good is a moral and civil man, is, because spiritual good has within itself the essence of good, and from this moral and civil good. The essence of good cannot come from any other source than from Him who is Good Itself. Give to thought its freest range, call forth all its powers, and inquire whence good is good, and you will see that it is from its *esse*,* and that that is good which has the *esse* of good in it, consequently, that that is good which is from Good Itself, thus from God; and therefore that good not from God, but from man, is not good.

14. From what has been said in the DOCTRINE CONCERNING THE SACRED SCRIPTURE, n. 27, 28, 38, it may be seen that the first, mediate, and last make one, like end, cause, and effect; and that because they make one, the end itself is called the primary end, the cause the mediate end, and the effect the last or ultimate end. Hence it will be evident, that with the man who is in spiritual good; moral good is mediate spiritual good, and civil good is lowest or ultimate spiritual good. Hence then

* It is impossible to express by any single word in our language, the precise idea which the author here means to convey by the word *esse*. The reader who is acquainted with the Latin language will readily apprehend the full meaning of the term; in order, however, to assist the conception of the unlearned, it may be well to observe, that the word *esse*,—literally signifying *to be*,—is used by the author to express the inmost principle or being of a thing. As applied here to good, it signifies good in its very inmost, which is God; and that nothing therefore is really good, but what has its inmost principle of goodness in God. The same term is applied below, n. 43 and 48, to the human will, as distinguished from the understanding; the understanding being an existence, whose *esse*, or ground of being, is in the will.

it is, that it was said that the man who is in spiritual good, is a moral man, and a civil man; and that the man who is not in spiritual good, is neither a moral nor a civil man, but only so appears. He appears so to himself and also to others.

15. The reason why a man who is not spiritual can yet think and thence speak rationally, like a spiritual man, is, because the understanding of man is capable of being elevated into the light of heaven, which is truth, and of seeing by that light, although the will may not be similarly elevated into the heat of heaven, which is love, and act from that heat. Hence it is, that truth and love do not make one with man, unless he be spiritual. Hence also it is that man has the faculty of speech; this also forms a distinction between man and beast. It is through this capacity of the understanding to be elevated into heaven while the will is not yet elevated, that man is capable of being reformed, and of becoming spiritual; but he is first reformed, and becomes spiritual, when the will also is elevated. It is from this capability of the understanding above the capacity of the will, that man, of whatsoever quality he may be, even though he be evil, is able to think, and thence to speak rationally, like a spiritual man. But that nevertheless he is not rational, is because the understanding does not lead the will, but the will the understanding; the understanding only teaches and points out the way, as was said in the DOCTRINE CONCERNING THE SACRED SCRIPTURE, n. 45. And so long as the will is not with the understanding in heaven, the man is not spiritual, and hence not rational; for when he is left to his own will, or his own love, he rejects the rational things of the understanding, concerning God, concerning heaven, and eternal life, and in their place assumes such things as harmonize with the love of his will, and calls them rational. But these subjects will be considered in the treatises concerning ANGELIC WISDOM.

16. In the following pages, those who do good from themselves will be called natural men, since with them moral and civil life as to its essence, is natural; but those who do good from the Lord will be called spiritual men, because moral and civil life with them as to its essence, is spiritual.

17. That no one can do any good, which is really good, from himself, the Lord teaches in John: "*A man can receive nothing, except it be given him from heaven*" (iii. 27). And again: "*He that abideth in me, and I in him, the same bringeth forth much fruit; for without me ye can do nothing*" (xv. 5). "He that abideth in me and I in him, the same bringeth forth much fruit," signifies, that all good is from the Lord; fruit signifies good. "Without me ye can do nothing," signifies, that no one can do good from himself. They who believe in the Lord, and do good from him, are called *sons of light* (John xii. 36; Luke xvi. 8); *sons of the marriage* (Mark ii. 19); *sons of the resur-*

rection (Luke xx. 36); *sons of God* (Luke xx. 36; John i. 12); *born of God* (John i. 13) ;—and it is said *that they shall see God* (Matt. v. 8); *that the Lord will make his abode with them* (John xiv. 23); *that they have the faith of God* (Mark xi. 22); *and that their works are done from God* (John iii. 21). These are all comprised in the words, "*As many as received Jesus, to them gave he power to become the sons of God, even to them that believe on his name; who were born, not of blood, nor of the will of the flesh, nor of the will of man, but of God*" (John i. 12, 13). To believe in the name of the Son of God, is to believe the Word, and to live according to it. The will of the flesh is the *proprium* of man's will, which in itself is evil; and the will of man is the *proprium* of his understanding, which in itself is falsity from evil. Those who are born of these, are such as will and act, and think and speak, from their *proprium;* those who are born of God, are such as do these things from the Lord. In short, that is not good which is from man, but that which is from the Lord.

III. THAT SO FAR AS A MAN SHUNS EVILS AS SINS, SO FAR HE DOES GOOD, NOT FROM HIMSELF, BUT FROM THE LORD.

18. Who does not know, or may not know, that evils prevent the Lord's entrance into man? For evil is hell, and the Lord is heaven, and hell and heaven are opposites. So far, therefore, as man is in the one, so far he cannot be in the other; for one acts against and destroys the other.

19. While man is in the world, he is in the midst between hell and heaven; beneath is hell, and above is heaven. And then he is kept in the freedom to turn himself either to hell or to heaven; if he turns himself to hell, he averts himself from heaven; on the other hand, if he turns himself to heaven, he averts himself from hell. Or, what is the same, while he is in the world, man is in the midst between the Lord and the devil, and is kept in freedom to turn himself either to the one or to the other; if he turns himself to the devil, he averts himself from the Lord; but if he turns himself to the Lord, he averts himself from the devil. Or, what is the same, while man lives in the world, he is in the midst between evil and good, and is kept in freedom to turn himself either to the one or to the other; if he turns himself to evil, he averts himself from good; but if he turns himself to good, he averts himself from evil.

20. It is said that man is kept in freedom to turn himself this way or that. Every man has this freedom not from himself, but from the Lord; wherefore it is said that he is *kept* in it.*

* Concerning the equilibrium between heaven and hell, and that man is in it, and thence in freedom, see the work on HEAVEN AND HELL, n. 589—596, and n. 597—603.

13

That every man is kept in freedom, and that it is taken away from no one, will be seen in its proper place.

21. From these considerations it is clear, that so far as man shuns evils, so far he is with the Lord, and in the Lord; and so far as he is in the Lord, so far he does good, not from himself but from the Lord. Hence results this general law : THAT SO FAR AS ANY ONE SHUNS EVILS, SO FAR HE DOES GOOD.

22. Two things however are required; one is, that a man should shun evils because they are sins,—that is, because they are infernal and diabolical, and thus opposed to the Lord, and contrary to the Divine laws. The other is, that a man should shun evils as sins as if from himself, and yet know and believe that he does so from the Lord. But these two requisites will be treated of in the following articles.

23. From what has been said these three consequences follow :—I. That if a man wills and does good before he shun sevils as sins, the good that he wills and does is not good. II. That if a man thinks pious thoughts and speaks pious words, and does not shun evils as sins, the pious things which he thinks and speaks are not pious. III. That if a man knows, and is wise in many things, and does not shun evils as sins, yet he is not wise.

24. I. *That if a man wills and does good before he shuns evils as sins, the good that he wills and does is not good.* This is because before that he is not in the Lord, as was said above. For example : if he gives to the poor, assists the needy, endows temples and hospitals, does good to the church, to his country, and his fellow-citizens, teaches the Gospel and converts souls, does justice in judgment, acts with sincerity in business, and with uprightness in his labor, and yet makes nothing of evils, as sins,—as the evils of fraud, adultery, hatred, blasphemy, and the like,—in this case he can do no other good than such as is inwardly evil; for he does it from himself, and not from the Lord. Thus he himself, and not the Lord, is in it; and the good actions in which man himself is are all defiled with his evils, and regard himself and the world. Yet these same actions that are enumerated above are inwardly good, if a man shuns evils as sins,—as the evils of fraud, adultery, hatred, blasphemy, and the like; for he does them from the Lord, and they are said to be *wrought in God* (John iii. 19—21).

25. II. *That if a man thinks pious thoughts and speaks pious words, and does not shun evils as sins, the pious things which he thinks and speaks are not pious.* The reason of this is because he is not in the Lord. For example : if he frequents places of public worship, attends devoutly to the preaching, reads the Word and books of piety, partakes of the sacrament of the Supper, offers up daily prayer,—yea, if he even thinks much about God, and about salvation, and yet makes nothing of evils

which are sins,—as the evils of fraud, adultery, hatred, blasphemy, and the like,—then the pious things which he thinks and speaks can be no other than such as are inwardly not pious; for the man himself with his evils is in them. This indeed he does not then know; but nevertheless they are therein, and lie hidden before him; for he is as a fountain whose water, from its very source and nature, is impure. His exercises of piety are either merely formal, from habit, or they are meritorious, or they are hypocritical. They ascend indeed towards heaven, but, like smoke in the air, turn back in their course, and fall down again.

26. It has been granted me to see and hear many after death who enumerated their good works and exercises of piety,—those which are mentioned above (n. 24, 25), and many besides. Among them I have seen some who had lamps and no oil; and inquiry was made whether they had shunned evils as sins. It was found that they had not; wherefore it was declared to them that they were evil. They were also afterwards seen to enter into caverns where there were similar evil spirits.

27. III. *That if a man knows, and is wise in many things, and does not shun evils as sins, yet he is not wise.* This is from a similar cause to that mentioned before, namely, because he is wise from himself, and not from the Lord. For example: if he understands the doctrine of his church, and has an accurate knowledge of all things relating to it; if he knows how to confirm this doctrine, by the Word, and by reasonings; if he knows the doctrines of all churches in all ages, and at the same time the decrees of all councils; nay, if he knows truths, and also sees and understands them,—thus, if he knows the nature of faith, charity, piety, repentance and the remission of sins, regeneration, baptism and the holy supper, the Lord, and redemption and salvation, still he is not wise if he does not shun evils as sins. For his knowledges are without life, because they are only of his understanding, and not at the same time of his will; and in this case they in time perish, for the reason given above (n. 15). Moreover after death the man himself rejects them, because they do not agree with the love of his will. And yet knowledges are in the highest degree necessary, because they teach how a man ought to act; and when he does them, then with him they live;—not before.

28. All that has been said hitherto is taught in the Word, in many places; of which the following only shall be adduced. The Word teaches that no one can be in good, and, at the same time, in evil; or what is the same, that no one, as to his soul, can be in heaven, and at the same time in hell. This is taught in these passages:—"*No man can serve two masters; for either he will hate the one and love the other, or else he will hold to the one and despise the other. Ye cannot serve God and mammon*".

(Matt. vi. 24). *" How can ye, being evil, speak good things ? for out of the abundance of the heart the mouth speaketh. A good man out of the good treasure of his heart bringeth forth good things, and an evil man out of the evil treasure bringeth forth evil things "* (Matt. xii. 34, 35). *" A good tree bringeth not forth corrupt fruit, neither doth a corrupt tree bring forth good fruit. Every tree is known by its fruit ; for of thorns men do not gather figs, nor of a bramble-bush gather they grapes "* (Luke vi. 43, 44).

29. The Word teaches, that no one can do good from himself, but from the Lord. Jesus said, *" I am the true vine, and my Father is the vinedresser ; every branch in me that beareth not fruit he taketh away ; and every branch that beareth fruit he will prune it, that it may bring forth more fruit. Abide in me, and I in you ; as the branch cannot bear fruit of itself, except it abide in the vine, no more can ye, except ye abide in me. I am the vine, ye are the branches ; he that abideth in me, and I in him, the same bringeth forth much fruit ; for without me ye can do nothing. If a man abide not in me, he is cast forth as a branch, and is withered, and men gather them, and cast them into the fire, and they are burned "* (John xv. 1, 2, 4—6).

30. The Word teaches, that so far as man is not purified from evils, his good deeds are not good, nor are his pious acts pious, neither is he wise ; and *vice versâ.* This is taught in these words : *" Woe unto you, Scribes and Pharisees, hypocrites ! for ye are like unto whited sepulchres, which indeed appear beautiful outwardly, but within are full of the bones of the dead, and all uncleanness ; even so ye, also, outwardly appear righteous unto men, but within ye are full of hypocrisy and iniquity "* (Matt. xxiii. 27, 28) ; *" Woe unto you, for ye make clean the outside of the cup and the platter, but within they are full of extortion and excess. Thou blind Pharisee ! cleanse first the inside of the cup and the platter, that the outside may be clean also "* (xxiii. 25, 26).

And also in these words from Isaiah : *" Hear the word of Jehovah, ye princes of Sodom ; give ear unto the law of our God, ye people of Gomorrah ! What to me is the multitude of your sacrifices ?—Bring no more an oblation of vanity : incense is an abomination unto me, the new moon and the sabbath :—I cannot bear iniquity.—Your new moons and your appointed feasts my soul hateth.—Wherefore when ye spread forth your hands, I will hide mine eyes from you ; yea, when ye make many prayers, I will not hear : your hands are full of bloods. Wash you, make you clean ; put away the evil of your doings from before mine eyes ; cease to do evil ;—though your sins be as scarlet, they shall be as white as snow ; though they be red like crimson, they shall be as wool "* (i. 10, 11, 13—18). The teaching of these words

16

briefly is, that unless a man shuns evils, none of his acts of worship and none of his works are good; for it is said, I cannot bear iniquity, make you clean, put away the evil of your doings, cease to do evil. So in Jeremiah: *"Return ye every man from his evil way, and make your works good"* (xxxv. 15).

That the same are not wise, is taught in Isaiah: *"Woe unto them that are wise in their own eyes, and intelligent before their own faces"* (v. 21). Again: *"The wisdom of the wise and the understanding of the intelligent shall perish. Woe unto them that are profoundly wise,—and their works are in the dark"* (xxix. 14, 15). And elsewhere in the same prophet: *"Woe unto them that go down into Egypt for help, and stay on horses, and trust in chariots because they are many, and in horsemen because they are strong; but they look not unto the Holy One of Israel, neither seek Jehovah! But He will arise against the house of the evil-doers, and against the help of them that work iniquity. For Egypt is man, and not God; and the horses thereof are flesh, and not spirit"* (xxxi. 1—3). Thus is described man's own intelligence: Egypt denotes science; the horse is understanding thence derived; the chariot is doctrine, and the horseman intelligence from thence;—of which it is said, "Woe unto them that do not look to the Holy One of Israel, and do not seek Jehovah." Their destruction by evils, is meant by the words, "He will arise against the house of the evil-doers, and against the help of them that work iniquity;" that these things are from the *proprium* of man, and therefore have no life in them, is meant by the declaration, that Egypt is man and not God, and that the horses thereof are flesh and not spirit. Man and flesh denote the *proprium* of man; God and spirit are life from the Lord; the horses of the Egyptians denote man's own intelligence. There are many such passages in the Word, concerning intelligence from self and intelligence from the Lord,—which are only explained by the spiritual sense.

That no one will be saved by means of good that he does from self, because it is not good, is clear from these passages: *"Not every one that saith unto me, Lord, Lord, shall enter into the kingdom of the heavens, but he that doeth the will of my Father.—Many will say unto me in that day, Lord, Lord, have we not prophesied in thy name, and in thy name cast out devils, and in thy name done many wonderful works? But then will I profess unto them, I never knew you; depart from me, YE THAT WORK INIQUITY"* (Matt. vii. 21—23). And in another place: *"Then shall ye begin to stand without, and to knock at the door, saying, Lord, open unto us.—And ye shall begin to say, We have eaten and drunk in thy presence, and thou hast taught in our streets. But He shall say, I tell you, I know you not whence ye are; depart from me, all ye WORKERS OF INIQUITY"* (Luke xiii. 25—27). For such persons are like the Pharisee, *who stood*

*in the temple and prayed, saying, that he was not as other men,
an extortioner, unjust, an adulterer; that he fasted twice in the
week, and gave tithes of all that he possessed* (Luke xviii. 11—
14). These, moreover, are they who are called *unprofitable
servants* (Luke xvii. 10).

31. It is a truth that no man can do good, which is really
good, from himself. But by this truth to destroy every good of
charity that a man does who shuns evils as sins, is an enormous
perversion; for it is diametrically opposed to the Word, which
enjoins that man shall do good. It is contrary to the commandments of love to God, and love towards the neighbour, on which
commandments hang all the law and the prophets, and it under-
mines and makes a mockery of all religion; for every one knows
that religion consists in doing good, and that every one will be
judged according to his deeds. Every man is so constituted that
he is able to shun evils, as of himself, by the power of the Lord,
if he implore it; and what he does after this is good from the
Lord.

IV. THAT SO FAR AS ANY ONE SHUNS EVILS AS SINS, SO FAR HE LOVES TRUTHS.

32. THERE are two universals which proceed from the Lord,
Divine Good and Divine Truth; Divine Good is of His Divine
Love, and Divine Truth is of His Divine Wisdom. These two
are one in the Lord, and thence as one proceed from Him; but
they are not received as one by the angels in heaven and by
men on earth. There are angels and men who receive more of
Divine Truth than of Divine Good; and there are those who
receive more of Divine Good than of Divine Truth. Hence it is
that the heavens are distinguished into two kingdoms, of which
one is called the celestial kingdom, and the other the spiritual
kingdom; the heavens which receive more of the Divine Good,
constitute the celestial kingdom, and those which receive more
of the Divine Truth constitute the spiritual kingdom.* But still
the angels of all the heavens are in wisdom and intelligence, in
the degree that good with them makes one with truth. The good
that does not make one with truth, to them is not good; and the
truth that does not make one with good, to them is not truth.
Hence it appears that good conjoined with truth constitutes love
and wisdom, with an angel and with man; and since an angel is
an angel by virtue of the love and wisdom that he has, and in
like manner a man is a man, it is evident, that good conjoined
with truth makes an angel to be an angel of heaven, and a man
to be a man of the church.

33. Since good and truth are one in the Lord, and proceed

---

* Concerning these two kingdoms, into which the heavens are distinguished,
see the work on HEAVEN AND HELL, n. 20—28.

as one from Him, it follows, that good loves truth, and truth loves good, and that they desire to be one.   The like is true of their opposites; evil loves falsity, and falsity loves evil, and they desire to be one.   In the following pages, the conjunction of good and truth will be called the heavenly marriage; and the conjunction of evil and falsity will be called the infernal marriage.

34. It follows from these considerations, that so far as any one shuns evils as sins, so far he loves truths; for so far he is in good, as was just shewn in the preceding article.   Then, on the other hand, so far as any one does not shun evils as sins, so far he does not love truths, because so far he is not in good.

35. A man who does not shun evils as sins, may indeed love truths; yet he does not love them because they are truths, but because they are serviceable to his reputation, whence he derives honor or gain.   Wherefore, if they do not serve this end, he does not love them.

36. Good is of the will; truth is of the understanding. From the love of good in the will proceeds the love of truth in the understanding; from the love of truth proceeds the perception of truth; from the perception of truth the thought of truth; and from these is the acknowledgment of truth, which is faith in its genuine sense.   That this is the order of progression from the love of good to faith, is shewn in the treatise on the DIVINE LOVE AND THE DIVINE WISDOM.

37. Since good is not good, as has been said, unless it be conjoined with truth, it follows that good does not before exist, although it continually wills to exist.   Wherefore, in order that it may exist, it desires and procures to itself truths; from these it derives its nourishment and formation.   This is the reason why, so far as any one is in good, so far he loves truths.   In like manner, so far as any one shuns evils as sins he loves truths; for so far he is in good.

38. So far as any one is in good, and from good loves truths, so far he loves the Lord, since the Lord is Good Itself and Truth Itself.   The Lord is therefore with man in good and in truth; if the latter be loved from the former, then the Lord is loved, and not otherwise.   This the Lord teaches in John: *"He that hath my precepts and doeth them, he it is that loveth me;—but he that loveth me not, keepeth not my words"* (xiv. 21, 24).   And in another place: *"If ye keep my commandments, ye shall abide in my love"* (John xv. 10).   The precepts, words, and commandments of the Lord are truths.

39. That good loves truth, may be illustrated by reference to the several cases of a priest, a soldier, a merchant, and an artificer.   First, a PRIEST: If he be in the good of the priesthood,—which is, to provide for the salvation of souls, to teach the way to heaven, and to lead those whom he teaches,—in the

degree that he is in that good, from love and its desire he procures to himself the truths that he teaches, and by which he leads. And a priest who is not in the good of the priesthood, but in the delight of his function from the love of self and of the world, which is his only good,—he also, from this love and its desire, procures to himself those truths, in abundance, according to the inspiring delight, which is its good. A SOLDIER: If he be in the love of military service, and is sensible of good in the protection of the state, or in his own fame, from that good, and according to it, he procures to himself the science of his profession; and if he be in command, its intelligence. These are as truths, by which the delight of his love, which is its good, is nourished and formed. A MERCHANT: If he has devoted himself to trade from the love of it, he imbibes with pleasure all things which, as means, enter into and compose that love; these also are as its truths, while trading is its good. An ARTIFICER: If he apply in good earnest to his occupation, and love it as the good of his life, he procures instruments, and perfects himself by such things as belong to the science of his art; by these means he causes his work to be good. From these cases it is evident, that truths are the means by which the good of love exists, and becomes a reality; consequently, that good loves truths in order that it may exist. Hence, in the Word, by doing the truth is meant, to cause good to exist. This is meant by *doing the truth*, in John iii. 21; by *doing the Lord's sayings*, in Luke vi. 47; by *keeping His precepts*, John xiv. 21; by *doing His words*, Matt. vii. 24; by *doing the word of God*, Luke viii. 21; and by *doing the statutes and judgments*, in Levit. xviii. 5. This also is meant by *doing good, and bearing fruit*; for good, or fruit, is that which exists.

40. That good loves truth, and wills to be conjoined with it, may also be illustrated by comparison with food and water, or with bread and wine. There must be the one as well as the other. Food or bread alone does not produce anything in the body for its nutrition, but with water or wine; wherefore the one seeks and desires the other. By food and bread, moreover, in the Word, in its spiritual sense, is meant good, and by water and wine is meant truth.

41. From what has been said, it is now evident, that he who shuns evils as sins, loves truths and desires them; and that the more he shuns evils as sins, so much the more he loves and desires truths, because he is so much the more in good. Hence he comes into the heavenly marriage, which is the marriage of good and truth,—in which heaven is, and in which the church will be.

V. THAT SO FAR AS ANY ONE SHUNS EVILS AS SINS, SO FAR HE HAS FAITH, AND IS SPIRITUAL.

42. FAITH and life are distinct from each other, like thinking and doing; and as thinking is of the understanding, and doing is of the will, it follows, that faith and life are distinct from each other, like the understanding and the will. He who knows the distinction between the latter, may know also the distinction between the former; and he who knows the conjunction of the latter, may also know the conjunction of the former; wherefore something concerning the understanding and the will shall be premised.

43. Man has two faculties, of which one is called the WILL and the other the UNDERSTANDING. They are distinct from each other, but are so created, that they may be one; and when they are one, they are called THE MIND. Wherefore these constitute the human mind, and all the life of man therein. As all things in the universe which are according to divine order relate to good and truth, so all things with man relate to the will and the understanding; for good with man is of his will, and truth with him is of his understanding. These two faculties, indeed, are the receptacles and subjects of those things; the will is the receptacle and subject of everything of good, and the understanding is the receptacle and subject of everything of truth. Goods and truths have no other abiding place with man;—so love and faith have no other abiding place; since love is of good, and good is of love, and faith is of truth, and truth is of faith. There is nothing of greater interest to know, than how the will and understanding make one mind. They make one mind as good and truth make one; for there is a similar marriage between the will and the understanding, as between good and truth. The nature of this marriage was shewn, in some degree, in the preceding article; to which this is to be added :· That as good is the very *esse* of a thing, and truth is the *existere* of a thing thence derived, so the will, with man, is the very *esse* of his life, and the understanding is the *existere* of his life, thence derived; for good, which is of the will, forms itself in the understanding, and, in a certain manner, makes itself visible.

44. It was shewn above (n. 27, 28), that a man may know, think, and understand many things, and yet not be wise; and since it is of faith to know and to think, and still more to understand that a thing is so, it is possible for a man to believe that he has faith, and yet have it not. The reason why he has it not is, because he is in the evil of life, and the evil of life and the truth of faith can never act as one. The evil of life destroys the truth of faith ;—because the evil of life is of the will, and the truth of faith is of the understanding, and the will leads the understanding, and causes it to act as one with itself.

21

Wherefore, if there is anything in the understanding that does not accord with the will, when man is left to himself, and thinks from his evil and its love, then the truth which is in the understanding he either rejects, or by falsification forces it into unity. It is otherwise with those who are in the good of life; they, when left to themselves, think from good, and the truth which is in the understanding they love, because it accords with the will. Thus there is effected a conjunction of faith and life, as there is a conjunction of truth and good; and each is like the conjunction of the understanding and the will.

45. Now from these considerations it follows, that in the degree that man shuns evils as sins he has faith, because in that degree he is in good, as was shewn above. This is confirmed also by its contrary, that he who does not shun evils as sins, has not faith, because he is in evil, and evil inwardly hates truth; outwardly, indeed, it may act as its friend, and endure, yea love, that truth should be in the understanding; but when the external is put off,—which it is after death,—then truth, its friend in the world, it first rejects, afterwards denies that it is the truth, and finally holds in aversion.

46. The faith of an evil man is intellectual faith, in which there is nothing of good from the will. Thus it is a dead faith, which is like the breathing of the lungs without its animation from the heart;—the understanding, moreover, corresponds to the lungs, and the will to the heart. It is also like a beautiful harlot, adorned even with purple and gold, who is inwardly full of malignant disease;—a harlot also corresponds to the falsification of truth, and hence signifies that in the Word. It is also like a tree abounding with leaves and yielding no fruit, which the gardener cuts down;—a tree likewise signifies man, its leaves and blossoms the truths of faith, and its fruit the good of love. But it is otherwise with faith in the understanding in which there is good from the will. This faith is alive, and is like the breathing of the lungs in which there is animation from the heart; and it is like a beautiful wife, whom chastity endears to her husband; it is also like a tree that bears fruit.

47. There are many truths which appear to be of faith only. As that there is a God; that the Lord, who is God, is the Redeemer and Saviour, that there is a heaven and a hell; that there is a life after death,—and many others; concerning which it is not said that they are to be done, but that they are to be believed. These truths of faith also are dead with the man who is in evil, but alive with the man who is in good. The reason is, because the man who is in good, not only does well from the will, but also thinks well from the understanding,—not merely before the world, but also before himself when he is alone. It is otherwise with him who is in evil.

48. It is said that these truths appear to be of faith only;

but the thought of the understanding derives its *existere* from the love of the will, which is the *esse* of the thought in the understanding, as was said above (n. 43). For whatever any one wills from love, that he wills to do, wills to think, wills to understand, and wills to speak; or, which is the same thing, what any one loves from the will, that he loves to do, loves to think, loves to understand, and loves to speak. It is to be added that when a man shuns evil as sin, then he is in the Lord, as was shewn above, and the Lord operates all things; where-fore, to those who asked Him, *what they should do, that they might work the works of God,* the Lord said, *"This is the work of God, that ye believe on Him whom he hath sent"* (John vi. 28, 29). To believe on the Lord, is not only to think that He is, but also to do His words, as He elsewhere teaches.

49. That those who are in evils have no faith, however they may suppose that they have, has been shewn by instances of such in the spiritual world. They were conducted to a heavenly society, whence the spiritual principle of the faith of the angels entered into the interiors of their faith; whereby they perceived that they had only a natural or external principle of faith, and not its spiritual or internal. Wherefore they themselves con-fessed that they had no faith; and that they had persuaded themselves in the world, that to believe, or to have faith, was to think that a thing is so, for any reason. But it was perceived to be otherwise with the faith of those who were not in evil.

50. From these considerations it may be seen what spiritual faith is, and what the faith is which is not spiritual;—that faith is spiritual with those who do not commit sins; for those who do not commit sins do good, not from themselves but from the Lord (as may be seen above, n. 18—31), and by faith become spiritual. Faith with them is truth. This the Lord thus teaches in John : *"This is the judgment, that light is come into the world, and men loved darkness rather than light, because their deeds were evil. For every one that doeth evil hateth the light, neither cometh to the light, lest his deeds should be re-proved; but he that doeth truth, cometh to the light, that his deeds may be made manifest, because they are wrought in God"* (iii. 19—21).

51. What has been said thus far is confirmed by the following passages from the Word : *"A good man, out of the good treasure of his heart, bringeth forth that which is good; and an evil man, out of the evil treasure of his heart, bringeth forth that which is evil; for of the abundance of the heart, his mouth speaketh"* (Luke vi. 45; Matt. xii. 35). By the heart in the Word is meant the will of man; and because from thence man thinks and speaks, it is said, out of the abundance of the heart the mouth speaketh. *"Not that which goeth into the mouth defileth a man, but that which cometh out of the mouth, this*

23

defileth the man.—*Those things which proceed out of the mouth come forth from the heart, and they defile the man"* (Matt. xv. 11, 18). By the heart here also is meant the will. *Jesus said concerning the woman who washed His feet with ointment, " Her sins are forgiven; for she loved much;" and afterwards He said, " Thy faith hath made thee whole"* (Luke vii. 47—50); from which it is evident, that when sins are remitted, that is, when they are not, faith saves. That they are called sons of God, and born of God, who are not in the *proprium* of their own will, and thence not in the *proprium* of their own understanding,—that is, who are not in evil and thence in falsity,—and that they are those who believe on the Lord, He Himself teaches in John i. 12, 13; which passages may be seen explained above (n. 17).

52. From these considerations the conclusion follows, that there is not with man a grain of truth, more than there is of good; thus not a grain of faith, more than there is of life. There is the thought in the understanding that a thing is so; but not the acknowledgment which is faith, unless there is consent in the will. Thus faith and life march on with equal step. From these observations it is now evident, that so far as any one shuns evils as sins, so far he has faith, and is spiritual.

VI. THAT THE DECALOGUE TEACHES WHAT EVILS ARE SINS.

53. WHAT nation on earth does not know that it is evil to steal, to commit adultery, to commit murder, and to bear false witness? If the nations did not know these things, and by laws prohibit such evils, they would come to destruction; for a society, commonwealth, or kingdom, without these laws would perish. Who can conceive that the Israelitish nation was, beyond all others, so senseless that they did not know that these things are evil? One may therefore wonder for what reason those laws, universally known on the earth, were so miraculously promulgated by Jehovah Himself from Mount Sinai. But listen. They were thus miraculously promulgated, that they might know that those laws are not only civil and moral laws, but also spiritual laws; and that to act contrary to them is not only to do evil against the citizen and against society, but is also to sin against God. Wherefore those laws, by their promulgation from Mount Sinai by Jehovah, were made the laws of religion; for it is evident that whatever Jehovah God commands, He commands in order that it may be a matter of religion, and that it ought to be done for His sake, and for man's salvation.

54. Those laws were so holy that nothing could be more holy;—because they were the first-fruits of the Word, and thence the first-fruits of the church which was about to be esta-

blished by the Lord with the people of Israel; and because they were, in a brief summary, a complex of all things of religion, by which conjunction is effected of the Lord with man, and of man with the Lord.

55. That they were most holy is evident from the fact that Jehovah Himself, that is, the Lord, descended upon Mount Sinai fire, and attended by angels, and thence promulgated them with the living voice;—and that, for three days the people prepared themselves to see and hear; that the mountain was fenced about, lest any one should approach and die; that neither the priests nor the elders were to come near, but Moses only; that those laws were written by the finger of God on two tables of stone; that the face of Moses shone when he brought them down a second time from the mountain; that they were afterwards deposited in the ark, and the ark in the inmost of the tabernacle, —and that over the ark was placed the mercy-seat, and above this cherubim of gold; that this inmost of the tabernacle was the most holy thing of their church, and was called the Holy of Holies; that without the vail, within which was this most holy place, were arranged the things which represented the holy things of heaven and of the church,—which were the candle-stick with the seven sconces of gold, the golden altar of incense, and the table overlaid with gold on which was the bread of faces, with the curtains of fine linen, purple, and scarlet round about. The sanctity of the whole tabernacle was from nothing else but from the law which was in the ark. On account of the holiness of the tabernacle, from the law in the ark, all the people of Israel, by command, encamped around it, in order according to their tribes, and marched in order after it; and then there was over it a cloud by day, and a fire by night. On account of the holiness of that law, and the presence of the Lord therein, the Lord talked with Moses from between the cherubim over the mercy-seat; and the ark was called Jehovah-There; more-over it was not lawful for Aaron to enter within the vail, except with sacrifices and incense. Because that law was the very sanctity of the Church, therefore the ark was introduced by David into Zion; and was afterwards deposited in the midst of the temple at Jerusalem, and constituted its inmost holy place. By reason of the presence of the Lord in that law, and around it, miracles were also wrought by the ark in which that law was contained;—as when the waters of Jordan were divided, and while the ark rested in the midst, the people passed over on dry ground; when the walls of Jericho fell down in consequence of its being carried around them; when Dagon, the god of the Philistines, fell down before it, and afterwards lay at the threshold of the temple, with the head separated from the body; and when the Bethshemites were smitten on account of it, to the number of many thousands; besides other miracles. These

25

were all from the presence of the Lord in His ten words, which are the commandments of the decalogue.

56. So great power and so great holiness were in that law, moreover, because it was the complex of all things of religion; for it consisted of two tables, of which one contains all things that are on the part of God, and the other all things in one complex that are on the part of man. Therefore, the precepts of that law are called the ten words; they are so called, because the number ten signifies all. But how that law is the complex of all things of religion, will be seen in the following article.

57. Because by means of that law there is conjunction of the Lord with man, and of man with the Lord, it is called the COVENANT, and the TESTIMONY,—the Covenant because it conjoins, and the Testimony because it testifies; for a covenant signifies conjunction, and a testimony the testification of it. It was on this account that there were two tables, one for the Lord, and the other for man. Conjunction is effected by the Lord,—but only when man does those things which are written in his table. For the Lord is continually present, and operative, and desirous to enter, but it is for man in the exercise of his freedom, which he has from the Lord, to open the door; for He says, "*Behold, I stand at the door and knock; if any man hear my voice, and open the door, I will come in to him, and will sup with him, and he with me*" (Rev. iii. 20).

58. In the other table, which is for man, it is not said that he should do this or that good, but that he should not do this or that evil;—as, Thou shalt not kill; Thou shalt not commit adultery; Thou shalt not steal; Thou shalt not bear false witness; Thou shalt not covet. The reason is, because man cannot do anything from himself; but when he does not do evils, then he does good, not from himself, but from the Lord. That man is able to shun evils as from himself, by the Lord's power if he implore it, will be seen in what follows.

59. What was stated above (n. 55), concerning the promulgation, holiness, and power of this law, may be found in the following passages in the Word.

That Jehovah descended upon Mount Sinai in fire, and that the mount then smoked and quaked; and that there were thunderings, lightnings, a thick cloud, and the voice of a trumpet, Exod. xix. 16, 18; Deut. iv. 11; v. 19—23.

That before the descent of Jehovah the people prepared and sanctified themselves for three days, Exod. xix. 10, 11, 15.

That the mountain was fenced about that no one might approach, and draw near to the foot of it, lest he should die; and that not even the priests, but Moses only should approach, Exod. xix. 12, 13, 20—23: xxiv. 1, 2.

The law, promulgated from Mount Sinai, Exod. xx. 2—17; Deut. v. 6—21.

26

That that law was written upon two tables of stone, with the finger of God, Exod. xxxi. 18; xxxii. 15, 16; Deut. ix. 10.

That when he brought those tables down from the mount the second time the face of Moses shone, Exod. xxxiv. 29—35.

That the tables were deposited in an ark, Exod. xxv. 16; xl. 20; Deut. x. 5; 1 Kings viii. 9.

That over the ark was the mercy-seat, and over this were placed cherubim of gold, Exod. xxxv. 17—21.

That the ark, with the mercy-seat and cherubim, formed the inmost of the tabernacle; and that the golden candlestick, the golden altar of incense, and the table overlaid with gold on which was the bread of faces, formed the exterior part of the tabernacle; and the ten curtains of fine linen, purple and scarlet, formed its outermost part; Exod. xxv. 1 to the end; xxvi. 1 to the end; xl. 17—28.

That the place where the ark was, was called the Holy of Holies, Exod. xxvi. 33.

That all the people of Israel encamped around the tabernacle in order according to their tribes, and journeyed in order after it, Numbers ii. 1 to the end.

That there was then over the tabernacle a cloud by day, and fire by night, Exodus xl. 38; Numb. ix. 15, 16 to the end; xiv. 14; Deut. i. 33.

That the Lord talked with Moses from over the ark, between the cherubim, Exod. xxv. 22; Numb. vii. 89.

That on account of the law within it, the ark was called Jehovah-There,—for when the ark went forward, Moses said, *Arise Jehovah*, and when it rested, *Return Jehovah*, Numb. x. 35, 36; and also 2 Sam. vi. 2; Psalm cxxxii. 7, 8.

That on account of the holiness of that law, it was not lawful for Aaron to enter within the vail, except with sacrifices and with the incense, Levit. xvi. 2—14.

That the ark was introduced by David into Zion with sacrifices and rejoicing, 2 Sam. vi. 1—19; and that then Uzzah died, because he touched it, verses 6, 7, of the same chapter.

That the ark was placed in the midst of the temple at Jerusalem, where it constituted the most holy place, 1 Kings vi. 19; viii. 3—9.

That by reason of the Lord's presence and power in the law which was in the ark, the waters of Jordan were divided, and, while the ark rested in the midst, the people passed over on dry ground, Josh. iii. 1—17; iv. 5—20.

That the walls of Jericho fell down in consequence of carrying the ark around them, Josh. vi. 1—20.

That Dagon the God of the Philistines fell to the earth before the ark, and afterwards lay at the threshold of the temple with the head separated from the body, 1 Sam. v. 3, 4.

27

That on account of the ark the Bethshemites were smitten, to the number of several thousands, 1 Sam. vi. 19.

60. That the tables of stone on which the law was written were called the tables of the covenant; and that the ark, on account of them, was called the ark of the covenant; and the law itself, the covenant, is taught in Numb. x. 33; Deut. iv. 13, 23; v. 2, 3; ix. 9; Josh. iii. 11; 1 Kings viii. 21; Rev. xi. 19; and many other places. The reason why the law was called the covenant, is because a covenant signifies conjunction; wherefore it is said concerning the Lord, that *He shall be for a covenant to the people* (Isaiah xlii. 6; xlix. 8); and He is called *the Angel of the covenant* (Mal. iii. 1); and His blood, *the blood of the covenant* (Matt. xxvi. 28; Zech. ix. 11; Exod. xxiv. 4—10). For the same reason the Word is called *the Old Covenant and the New Covenant.* Covenants, moreover, are made for the sake of love, of friendship, of consociation,—and thus of conjunction.

61. That the precepts of that law were called the ten words, appears from Exod. xxxiv. 28; Deut. iv. 13; x. 4.* They are so called, because the number ten signifies all, and words signify truths; for there were more than ten. Because the number ten signifies all, there were ten curtains of the tabernacle (Exod. xxvi. 1); therefore the Lord said, that a man about to receive a kingdom called ten servants, and gave them ten minas to trade with (Luke xix. 13); and therefore the Lord likened the kingdom of the heavens to ten virgins (Matt. xxv. 1). For the same reason the dragon is described as having ten horns (Rev. xii. 3); likewise the beast coming up out of the sea (Rev. xiii. 1); and also another beast (Rev. xvii. 3, 7); as well as the beast in Daniel (vii. 7, 20, 24). The like is signified by ten in Levit. xxvi. 26; Zech. viii. 23; and elsewhere. Hence there are tenths (tithes), by which is signified something from all.

VII. THAT MURDERS, ADULTERIES, THEFTS, AND FALSE WITNESS, OF EVERY KIND, WITH THE CONCUPISCENCES PROMPTING TO THEM, ARE EVILS WHICH ARE TO BE SHUNNED AS SINS.

62. It is known, that the law of Sinai was written upon two tables, and that the first table contains those things which relate to God, and the second, those which relate to man. That the first table contains all things which relate to God, and the second, all things which relate to man, does not appear in the letter; yet all things are therein, and therefore they are called the ten words,—by which are signified all truths in the complex, as may be seen just above (n. 61). But how all things are therein cannot be explained in a few words; it may, however, be comprehended from what was adduced in the DOCTRINE

---

* See the margin of the English Bible.

CONCERNING THE SACRED SCRIPTURE, n. 67, which see. Hence it is, that it is said, murders, adulteries, thefts, and false witness, of every kind.

63. A religious persuasion has prevailed, that no one can fulfil the law;—and the law is, not to kill, not to commit adultery, not to steal, and not to bear false witness. These precepts of the law every civil and moral man can fulfil as requirements of civil and moral life; but that he can fulfil them from a principle of spiritual life this persuasion denies. From this it follows, that he is to abstain from doing these evils only to avoid punishments and losses in the world, and not to avoid punishments and losses after he has left the world. Hence it is that the man with whom the above religious persuasion prevails thinks these evils lawful in the sight of God, but unlawful in the sight of the world. On account of this thought, from this his religion, the man remains in the concupiscence prompting to all these evils; and only refrains from doing them on account of the world. Wherefore such a man after death, although he had not committed murder, adultery, theft, and false witness, is still in the lust to commit them,—and also does commit them, when the external, which he had in the world, is removed from him; for all concupiscence remains with man after death. Hence it is, that such persons act in unity with hell, and cannot but have their portion with those who are in hell. But another lot awaits those who determine not to kill, to commit adultery, to steal, and to bear false witness, because to do these things is against God. After some combat against these evils, they do not incline to them, consequently do not desire to do them,— saying in their hearts that they are sins, in themselves infernal and diabolical. These, after death, when the external which they had for the world is removed, act in unity with heaven; and because they are in the Lord, they are also admitted into heaven.

64. It is a common maxim, in every religion, that man ought to examine himself, to do the work of repentance, and to abstain from sins; and that if he does not, he is in a state of condemnation. That this is common to every religion, may be seen above (n. 4—8). It is also a common practice in the whole Christian world to teach the decalogue, and thereby to initiate children into the Christian religion; for it is in the hands of all children as they advance towards youth. Their parents and masters tell them, that to do the evils therein forbidden is to sin against God; yea, while they are talking with the children, the parents and masters understand no otherwise. Who may not wonder that the same parents and masters, and also the children when they become adults, think that they are not under that law, and that they cannot do the things prescribed in that law! Can there be any other reason why they learn thus to

think, than that they love evils, and hence the falsities which favor them? These therefore are they who do not make the precepts of the decalogue precepts of religion. That the same live without religion, may be seen in the Doctrine concerning Faith.

65. Among all the nations on earth, with whom there is any religion, there are similar precepts to those in the decalogue; and all who live according to them, from a religious principle, are saved; and all who do not live according to them, from a religious principle, are condemned. Those who live according to them from a religious principle, being instructed after death by the angels, receive truths, and acknowledge the Lord. The reason is, because they shun evils as sins, and hence are in good,—and good loves truth, and from the desire of its love receives it; as was shewn above (n. 32—41). This is meant by the Lord's words to the Jews: *"The kingdom of God shall be taken from you, and given to a nation bringing forth the fruits thereof"* (Matt. xxi. 43); and also by these words: *"When the Lord of the vineyard cometh,—He will destroy the wicked, and will let out His vineyard unto other husbandmen, who shall render Him the fruits in their season"* (Matt. xxi. 40, 41); and by these: *"I say unto you, that many shall come from the east and the west, and from the north and the south, and shall sit down—in the kingdom of God; but the sons of the kingdom shall be cast out into outer darkness"* (Matt. viii. 11, 12; Luke xiii. 29).

66. We read in Mark, that a certain rich man came to Jesus, and asked Him, what he should do to inherit eternal life? To whom Jesus replied, *"Thou knowest the commandments: Thou shalt not commit adultery; thou shalt not kill; thou shalt not steal; thou shalt not bear false witness; defraud not; honor thy father and mother. He answering said, All these have I kept from my youth. Jesus looked upon him and loved him; and He said, One thing thou lackest; go thy way, sell whatsoever thou hast, and give to the poor, and thou shalt have treasure in heaven; and come, take up the cross, and follow me"* (x. 17—22). It is said that Jesus loved him; this was because he said that he had kept the commandments from his youth. But because he lacked three things,—which were, that he had not removed his heart from riches, that he had not fought against concupiscences, and that he had not yet acknowledged the Lord to be God,—therefore the Lord said, that he should sell all that he had, by which is meant, that he should remove his heart from riches; that he should take up the cross,—by which is meant, that he should fight against concupiscences; and that he should follow Him,—by which is meant, that he should acknowledge the Lord to be God. (The Lord spoke on this occasion, as on all others, by correspondences. See the Doctrine concerning the Sacred Scripture, n. 17.) For no one can shun evils as

sins, unless he acknowledge the Lord, and approach Him; and unless he fight against evils, and thus remove concupiscences. But more will be said on these subjects, in the article concerning combats against evils.

VIII. THAT SO FAR AS ANY ONE SHUNS MURDERS, OF EVERY KIND, AS SINS, SO FAR HE HAS LOVE TOWARDS THE NEIGHBOUR.

67. By murders of every kind are understood also every kind of enmity, hatred, and revenge, which breathe the spirit of murder; for in these murder lies concealed, as fire in wood beneath the ashes. Infernal fire is nothing else; and hence come the expressions, to be inflamed with anger, to burn with revenge. These are murders in the natural sense. But by murders, in the spiritual sense, are meant all modes of killing and destroying the souls of men; which are various and manifold. And by murder, in the supreme sense, is meant to have hatred towards the Lord. These three kinds of murders make one, and cohere; for whoever desires to kill the body of man in the world, has a disposition also to kill his soul after death; and he desires the destruction of the Lord,—for he burns with anger against Him, and wills to put out His name.

68. These kinds of murder lie inwardly concealed in man from his birth; but he learns even from infancy to cover them over with a veil of civility and morality,—which he must needs put on among men in the world,—and so far as he loves honor or gain, he is watchful, lest they appear. This is done in the external of man, while these are his internal. Such is man in himself. Now since he lays aside the external, with the body, when he dies, and retains the internal, it is evident what a devil he would be unless he were reformed.

69. Since the kinds of murders above mentioned lie inwardly concealed in man, as has been said, from his birth, and at the same time thefts of every kind, and false witness of every kind, with the concupiscences prompting to them,—concerning which something will be said below,—it is evident, that unless the Lord had provided the means of reformation, man could not but eternally perish. The means of reformation which the Lord has provided are these:—That man is born in mere ignorance; that while an infant he is kept in a state of external innocence; a little after, in a state of external charity; and then in a state of external friendship;—but as he comes into the exercise of thought from his own understanding, he is kept in a certain freedom of acting according to reason. This is the state which was described above (n. 19); and the description shall be here repeated, on account of what follows.

" While man is in the world, he is in the midst between hell and heaven; beneath is hell, and above is heaven. And then he is kept in freedom to turn himself either to hell or to heaven; if he turns himself to hell, he averts himself from heaven; on the other hand, if he turns himself to heaven, he averts himself from hell. Or, what is the same, while he is in the world, man is in the midst between the Lord and the devil, and is kept in freedom to turn himself either to the one or to the other; if he turns himself to the devil, he averts himself from the Lord; but if he turns himself to the Lord, he averts himself from the devil. Or, what is the same, while man lives in the world, he is in the midst between evil and good, and is kept in freedom to turn himself either to the one or to the other; if he turns himself to evil, he averts himself from good; but if he turns himself to good, he averts himself from evil." This is n. 19, above. See also n. 20—22, which there follow.

70. Now, as evil and good are two opposites,—precisely like heaven and hell, or like the devil and the Lord,—it follows, that if man shuns evil as sin, he comes into the good that is opposite to the evil. The good opposite to the evil which is understood by murder, is the good of neighbourly love.

71. Since this good and that evil are opposites, it follows that the latter is removed by the former. Two opposites cannot exist together; as heaven and hell cannot exist together. If they were together they would be lukewarm; concerning which state it is thus written in the Revelation, "*I know that thou art neither cold nor hot; I would thou wert cold or hot; but because thou art lukewarm, and neither cold nor hot, I will spue thee out of my mouth*" (iii. 15, 16).

72. When man is no longer in the evil of murder, but in the good of love towards the neighbour, then whatever he does is a good of that love; consequently it is a good work. A priest who is in that good, as often as he teaches and leads, does a good work, because he acts from the love of saving souls. A magistrate who is in that good, as often as he decides and judges, does a good work, because he acts from the love of caring for his country, for society, and for his fellow-citizens. A merchant, likewise, if he be in that good, every one of his transactions is a good work; there is in it the love of the neighbour,—and his country, society, his fellow-citizens, and also his servants are the neighbour, whose welfare he considers together with his own. A labourer, also, who is in that good, works faithfully under its influence, for others as for himself, fearing his neighbour's loss as his own. The reason why their deeds are good works is, that so far as any one shuns evil so far he does good, according to the general law above stated (n. 21); and he who shuns evil as sin, does good, not from himself, but from the Lord (n. 18—31). It is the very opposite with him who does not regard these kinds of murder—enmities, hatreds, revenge, and the like—as sins; whether he be a priest, a magistrate, a

merchant, or a laborer, whatever he does is not a good work, because his every work partakes of the evil that is within him. For it is his internal that produces; the external may be good, but only for others, not for himself.

73. The Lord teaches the good of love in many places in the Word. He teaches it, by reconciliation with the neighbour, in Matthew: "*If thou offerest thy gift upon the altar, and there rememberest that thy brother hath ought against thee, leave there thy gift before the altar, and go thy way; first be reconciled to thy brother, and then come and offer thy gift. Be well-minded to thine adversary, whilst thou art in the way with him; lest the adversary deliver thee to the judge, and the judge deliver thee to the officer, and thou be cast into prison. Verily, I say unto thee, Thou shalt not come out thence until thou hast paid the uttermost farthing*" (v. 23—26). It is evident that to be reconciled to a brother is to shun enmity, hatred, and revenge; that is, to shun them as sins. The Lord also teaches in Matthew, "*All things whatsoever ye would that men should do to you, do ye even so to them, for this is the law and the prophets*" (vii. 12): thus, that we should not do evil. The same is frequently taught in other places. The Lord also teaches, that even to be rashly angry with a brother, or with the neighbour, and to account him an enemy, is murder (Matt. v. 21, 22).

IX. THAT SO FAR AS ANY ONE SHUNS ADULTERIES OF EVERY KIND, AS SINS, SO FAR HE LOVES CHASTITY.

74. To commit adultery, in the sixth commandment of the decalogue, in the natural sense, means not only to commit fornication, but also to do obscene acts, to speak lascivious words, and to think unclean thoughts. But in the spiritual sense, to commit adultery means to adulterate the goods of the Word, and to falsify its truths. And in the supreme sense, to commit adultery means to deny the divinity of the Lord, and to profane the Word. These are adulteries of every kind. The natural man may know from rational light, that to commit adultery means also to do obscene acts, to speak lascivious words, and to think unclean thoughts; but he does not know, that to commit adultery also means to adulterate the goods of the Word, and to falsify its truths; and still less that it means to deny the divinity of the Lord, and to profane the Word. Hence he does not know, that adultery is so great an evil that it may be called utterly diabolical; for whoever is in natural adultery is also in spiritual adultery, and *vice versâ*. That this is the case will be shewn in a little special work on MARRIAGE.*

---

* The Author undoubtedly here refers to the work on CONJUGIAL LOVE, which was published some years later.—[Tr.]

But they are at the same time in adulteries of every kind, who do not regard adulteries as sins, in faith and life.

75. That so far as any one shuns adultery so far he loves marriage, or what is the same, so far as any one shuns the lasciviousness of adultery so far he loves the chastity of marriage, is because the lasciviousness of adultery and the chastity of marriage are two opposites; so far therefore as a man is not in the one so far he is in the other. It is altogether as was said above, n. 70.

76. No one can know what the chastity of marriage is unless he shuns the lasciviousness of adultery as sin. A man may know that in which he is, but he cannot know that in which he is not. If he know anything in which he is not, by description, or by thinking about it, yet he only knows it as in the shade, and uncertainty inheres; thus he does not see it in the light, and free from doubt, as when he is in it. This, therefore, is to know; but that is to know and not know. The truth is, that the lasciviousness of adultery and the chastity of marriage are to each other altogether as hell and heaven; and that the lasciviousness of adultery makes hell with man, and the chastity of marriage makes heaven with him. But the chastity of marriage is with no others than those who shun the lasciviousness of adultery as sin.*

77. From these considerations it may be concluded and seen, without doubt, whether a man is a Christian or not; yea, whether he has any religion or not. He who does not regard adulteries as sins, in faith and life, is not a Christian; nor has he any religion. But, on the other hand, he who shuns adulteries as sins, especially if on that account he is averse to them, and still more he who abominates them on that account, has religion; and if he be in the Christian church, he is a Christian. But concerning these things more will be said in the little work on MARRIAGE. But in the meantime see what is said on the subject in the work on HEAVEN AND HELL (n. 366—386).

78. That to commit adultery means also to do obscene acts, to speak lascivious words, and to think unclean thoughts, is evident from the Lord's words in Matthew: " *Ye have heard that it was said by them of old time, Thou shalt not commit adultery; but I say unto you, That whosoever looketh on a woman to lust after her, hath committed adultery with her already in his heart*" (v. 27, 28).

79. That in the spiritual sense to commit adultery means to adulterate the good of the Word, and to falsify its truth, is evident from these passages: " *Babylon—hath made all nations drink of the wine of her fornication*" (Rev. xiv. 8). *The angel said, I will shew thee the judgment of the great whore that*

---

* See below, n. 111.

sitteth upon many waters, with whom the kings of the earth have committed fornication (Rev. xvii. 1, 2). *"All nations have drunk of the wine of the wrath of her fornication, and the kings of the earth have committed fornication with her"* (Rev. xviii. 3). *God hath judged the great whore, which did corrupt the earth with her fornication* (Rev. xix. 2). Fornication is spoken of in relation to Babylon, because by Babylon are meant those who arrogate to themselves the divine power of the Lord, and profane the Word by adulterating and falsifying it; wherefore Babylon is also called *"the mother of fornications and abominations of the earth"* (Rev. xvii. 5). The same is signified by whoredom in the prophets. As in Jeremiah: *"I have seen in the prophets of Jerusalem a horrible thing; they commit adultery and walk in lies"* (xxiii. 14). And in Ezekiel: *"Two women, the daughters of one mother, committed whoredom in Egypt, they committed whoredom in their youth; one committed whoredom under me; and she doted on her lovers, on the Assyrians her neighbours; she bestowed her whoredoms upon them;—yet she forsook not her whoredoms in Egypt.—The other corrupted her love more than the former, and her whoredoms were more than the whoredoms of her sister: she increased her whoredoms, she loved the Chaldeans; the sons of Babel came to her to the bed of love, and defiled her by their whoredom"* (xxiii. 2—17). These words relate to the Israelitish and the Jewish church, which are here called the daughters of one mother. By their whoredoms are meant the adulterations and falsifications of the Word; and as in the Word Egypt signifies science, Assyria reasoning, Chaldea the profanation of truth, and Babylon the profanation of good, therefore it is said that they committed whoredom with them. The same is said in Ezekiel concerning Jerusalem, by which is signified the church as to doctrine: *"Thou didst trust in thy beauty, and didst commit whoredom because of thy renown, so that thou pouredst out thy whoredoms on every one that passed by.—Thou hast committed whoredom with the sons of Egypt thy neighbours, great of flesh, and hast multiplied thy whoredom.—Thou hast committed whoredom with the sons of Assyria; when thou wast not satisfied with those with whom thou didst commit whoredom, thou didst multiply thy whoredom even to Chaldea the land of merchandize. An adulterous wife hath received strangers instead of her husband; all give a reward to their whores, but thou hast given rewards to all thy lovers that come to thee in thy circuit for thy whoredoms. Wherefore, O harlot, hear the Word of Jehovah"* (xvi. 15, 26, 28, 29, 32, 33, 35). That by Jerusalem is meant the church may be seen, in the Doctrine concerning the Lord (n. 62, 63). Whoredoms have the same signification in Isaiah xxiii. 17, 18; lvii. 3; in Jeremiah iii. 2, 6, 8, 9,; v. 7; xiii. 27; xxix. 23; in Micah i. 7; in Nahum iii. 4; in Hosea iv. 10, 11; in Levit. xx. 5; in

Numbers xiv. 33; xv. 39; and in other places. On account of this signification the Jewish nation was called by the Lord *an adulterous generation*" (Matt. xii. 39; xvi. 4; Mark viii. 38).

X. THAT SO FAR AS ANY ONE SHUNS THEFTS, OF EVERY KIND, AS SINS, SO FAR HE LOVES SINCERITY.

80. To steal, in the natural sense, means not only to commit theft and robbery, but also to defraud, and under any pretence to take away the goods of another. But to steal, in the spiritual sense, means to deprive another of the truths of his faith, and of the goods of his charity. And in the supreme sense, to steal means to take away from the Lord that which is His, and attribute it to one's self, and thus to claim righteousness and merit. These are thefts of every kind; and they also make one, as do adulteries of every kind, and murders of every kind, spoken of above. That they make one, is, because one kind is involved in the other.

81. The evil of theft enters more deeply into man than any other evil, because it is conjoined with cunning and deceit; and cunning and deceit insinuate themselves even into the spiritual mind of man, wherein is his thought with the understanding. That man has a spiritual mind and a natural mind will be seen below.

82. The reason why so far as any one shuns theft as sin he loves sincerity, is that theft is also fraud, and fraud and sincerity are two opposites; so far, therefore, as any one is not in fraud, he is in sincerity.

83. By sincerity is also meant integrity, justice, fidelity, and uprightness. Man cannot be in these virtues of himself, so that he loves them from and for the sake of them; but whoever shuns fraud, cunning, and deceit, as sins, he is thus in them, not from himself but from the Lord, as was shewn above (n. 18—31). It is so with the priest, the magistrate, the judge, the merchant, the laborer, and with every one in his office and in his employment.

84. This the Word teaches, in many places; from which the following passages are adduced: "*He that walketh in righteousness and speaketh right things; he that despiseth oppressions for gain, that shaketh his hands from holding a bribe; that stoppeth his ears from the hearing of bloods, and shutteth his eyes from seeing evil; he shall dwell on high*" (Isaiah xxxiii. 15, 16). "*Jehovah, who shall abide in thy tabernacle, who shall dwell in the mountain of thy holiness? He that walketh uprightly and doeth righteousness;—he that backbiteth not with his tongue, nor doeth evil to his neighbour*" (Psalm xv. 1—3). "*Mine eyes shall be upon the faithful of the land, that they may dwell with me; he*

36

*that walketh in the way of the upright, he shall serve me.   He
that worketh deceit shall not dwell within my house; he that
speaketh lies shall not stand in my sight.   In the morning I will
cut off all the wicked of the land, that I may cut off from the
city all the workers of iniquity"* (Psalm ci. 6—8).

That if a man be not inwardly sincere, just, faithful, and
upright, he is even insincere, unjust, unfaithful, and without
uprightness, the Lord teaches in these words: *"Except your
righteousness shall exceed the righteousness of the scribes and
Pharisees, ye shall not enter into the kingdom of the heavens"*
(Matt. v. 20).   By righteousness that exceeds the righteousness
of the scribes and Pharisees is meant interior righteousness, in
which the man is who is in the Lord.   That man may be in
the Lord, He Himself also teaches in John: *"The glory which
thou gavest me I have given them, that they may be one even as
we are one; I in them, and thou in me, that they may be perfect
in one;—and that the love wherewith thou hast loved me may be
in them, and I in them"* (xvii. 22, 23, 26).   From this it is
evident, that they are perfect when the Lord is in them.   These
are they who are called *the pure in heart, who shall see God;
and the perfect as their Father in the heavens* (Matt. v. 8, 48).

85. It was said above (n. 81) that the evil of theft enters
more deeply into man than any other evil, because it is conjoined
with cunning and deceit; and cunning and deceit insinuate
themselves even into the spiritual mind of man, wherein is his
thought with the understanding.   Something shall now be said,
therefore, concerning the MIND of man.   That his understanding and will together constitute the mind of man may be seen
above (n. 43).

86. Man has a natural mind and a spiritual mind; the
natural mind is beneath, and the spiritual mind is above; the
natural mind is the mind of his world, and the spiritual mind is
the mind of his heaven.*   The natural mind may be called the
animal mind, and the spiritual mind the human mind.   By this
fact, that he has a spiritual mind, moreover, a man is distinguished from an animal.   By means of this he is capable of
being in heaven while he is in the world.   It is by means of
this also that man lives after death.

As to his understanding man may be in his spiritual mind,
and thence in heaven; but as to his will he cannot be in his spi-

---

* It was a doctrine among the ancient philosophers, that man is a *microcosm*,
or little world; in which the great world is portrayed in miniature. Thus, as
in the great world there is an inward or spiritual world, and an outward or
natural world, so it is with the little world of man; his inward or spiritual part
is what is here called his heaven, and his outward or natural part is called his
world. Each of these parts has its respective mind, or ruling spirit; and it is
according to this idea, that man's natural mind is here called the mind of his
world, or outward part, and his spiritual mind, the mind of his heaven, or of
his inward part.

ritual mind, and thence in heaven, unless he shuns evils as sins.
And if he be not in heaven as to his will also, he is still not in
heaven; for the will draws the understanding downwards, and
causes it to be equally animal and natural with itself.

Man may be compared to a garden, the understanding to
light, and the will to heat. In the winter time a garden is in
light and not at the same time in heat; but in the time of
summer it is in light and heat together. And thus a man who
is only in the light of the understanding is like a garden in the
time of winter; but he who is in the light of the understanding
and at the same time in the warmth of the will is like a garden
in time of summer. Moreover, the understanding is wise
from spiritual light, and the will loves from spiritual heat; for
spiritual light is the Divine Wisdom, and spiritual heat is the
Divine Love.

So long as a man does not shun evils, as sins, the concupiscences of evils obstruct the interiors of the natural mind on the
part of the will,—which are as a thick veil there, and like a
black cloud beneath the spiritual mind,—and prevent its being
opened. But as soon as a man shuns evils as sins, then the
Lord flows in from heaven, and removes the veil, and disperses
the cloud, and opens the spiritual mind, and thus introduces
him into heaven.

So long as the concupiscences of evils obstruct, as was said,
the interiors of the natural mind, so long man is in hell; but as
soon as these concupiscences are dispersed by the Lord, man is
in heaven. Again, so long as the concupiscences of evils
obstruct the interiors of the natural mind, so long he is a
natural man; but as soon as these concupiscences are dispersed
by the Lord he is a spiritual man. And again, so long as the
concupiscences of evils obstruct the interiors of the natural
mind, so long man is an animal,—differing only in that he has the
ability to think and speak, even of such things as he does not see
with his eyes, which he derives from the faculty of elevating the
understanding into the light of heaven; but as soon as these concupiscences are dispersed by the Lord man is a man, because
then he thinks truth in the understanding, from good in the will.
Lastly, so long as the concupiscences of evils obstruct the interiors of the natural mind, so long man is like a garden in time
of winter; but as soon as these concupiscences are dispersed by
the Lord, he is like a garden in the time of summer.

The conjunction of the will and the understanding in man
is meant in the Word by the heart and soul, and by the heart
and spirit. As where it is said, that God should be loved with
all the heart, and with all the soul (Matt. xxii. 37); and that
God would give a new heart, and a new spirit (Ezek. xi. 19;
xxxvi. 26, 27). By the heart is meant the will and its love; and
by the soul and the spirit, the understanding and its wisdom.

38

XI. THAT SO FAR AS ANY ONE SHUNS FALSE WITNESS, OF EVERY KIND, AS SIN, SO FAR HE LOVES TRUTH.

87. To bear false witness, in the natural sense, means not only to give false testimony, but also to lie and to defame. In the spiritual sense, to bear false witness means, to say and to persuade that falsity is truth, and that evil is good, and *vice versâ*. And in the supreme sense, to bear false witness, means to blaspheme the Lord and the Word. These are false witness in the threefold sense. That they make one with the man who testifies falsely, lies, and defames, may appear from what was said in the DOCTRINE CONCERNING THE SACRED SCRIPTURE (n. 5—7 *seq.* and n. 57) respecting the threefold sense of all that is contained in the Word.

88. As falsehood and truth are two opposites, it follows, that so far as any one shuns falsehood as sin, so far he loves truth.

89. So far as any one loves truth, so far he desires to know it, and is affected in heart when he finds it; nor can any other attain to wisdom. And so far as he loves to do the truth, so far he is sensible of the pleasantness [*amoenitas*] of the light in which truth is. It is the same in the case of the other virtues hitherto spoken of; as with the virtue of sincerity and justice with him who shuns thefts of every kind, chastity and purity with him who shuns adulteries of every kind, and love and charity with him who shuns murders of every kind, and so on. But he who is in their opposites, knows nothing of them, although everything is in them.

90. It is truth which is meant by seed in the field, concerning which the Lord thus speaks: "*A sower went forth to sow, and as he sowed some fell by the way-side, and it was trodden under foot, and the fowls of heaven devoured it; and some fell upon stony ground, but as soon as it was sprung up, because it had no root it withered away; and some fell among thorns, and the thorns sprang up with it and choked it; and other fell upon good ground, and sprang up, and bare fruit, a hundredfold*" (Luke viii. 5—8; Matt. xiii. 3—8; Mark iv. 3—8). The sower here is the Lord, and the seed is His Word, thus truth; the seed by the way-side is with those who do not care about truth; the seed upon stony ground is with those who are concerned about truth, but not for its own sake, thus not interiorly; the seed among thorns is with those who are in the concupiscences of evil; but the seed in good ground is with those who from the Lord love the truths which are in the Word, and from Him do them, and thus bear fruit. That these things are meant, appears from the explication of these words by the Lord (Matt. xiii. 19—23; Mark iv. 14—20; Luke viii. 11—15). From these expositions it is evident, that the truth of the Word cannot take root with those who have no care about truth; nor

with those who love truth outwardly and not inwardly; nor
with those who are in the concupiscences of evil; but with
those in whom the concupiscences of evil have been dispersed
by the Lord. With these, the seed, that is, the truth, takes
root in their spiritual mind; concerning which see above, n. 86,
at the end.

91. It is a common opinion at this day, that salvation consists in believing this or that which the church teaches; and
that salvation does not consist in doing the commandments of
the decalogue,—which are, not to kill, not to commit adultery,
not to steal, not to bear false witness, both in a restricted and
in an extended sense. For it is said, that works are not re-
garded by God, but faith; when, in fact, so far as any one is in
those evils, so far he is without faith,—as may be seen above (n.
42—52). Consult your reason, and consider whether any mur-
derer, adulterer, thief, and false witness can have faith, so long
as he is in the concupiscence of these evils; and then, whether
the concupiscence of these evils can be otherwise dispersed,
than by willing not to do them, because they are sins, that is,
because they are infernal and diabolical. Whoever, therefore,
supposes that the way to be saved is to believe this or that
which the church teaches, and is still of such a character, cannot but be foolish, according to the words of the Lord in
Matthew vii. 26.   Such a church is thus described in Jeremiah:
*" Stand in the gate of the house of Jehovah, and proclaim there
this word :—Thus saith Jehovah of Hosts, the God of Israel,
Amend your ways and your works :—Trust ye not in the words
of a lie, saying, The temple of Jehovah, the temple of Jehovah,
the temple of Jehovah, are these.—Will ye steal, murder, and
commit adultery, and swear by a lie,—and come and stand before
me in this house, which is called by my name, and say, We are
delivered, while ye do these abominations ? Is this house become
a den of robbers ?—Yet I, behold I have seen, saith Jehovah"*
(vii. 2—4, 9—11).

XII. THAT NO ONE CAN SHUN EVILS AS SINS, SO AS INWARDLY TO HOLD THEM IN AVERSION, EXCEPT BY COMBATS AGAINST THEM.

92. Every one may know from the Word, and by doctrine
from the Word, that the *proprium* of man is evil from his
birth; and that hence it is that from innate concupiscence he
loves evils, and is brought into them,—so that he wills to
revenge, to defraud, to defame, and to commit adultery. And
if he does not consider that these evils are sins, and on that
account resist them, he does them as often as occasion presents
itself and his interest and reputation are not endangered. It

is to be added, that if a man is without religion he does these things from delight.

93. Since this *proprium* of man constitutes the first root of his life, it is evident what sort of a tree man would be if this root were not extirpated, and a new root implanted. He would be a rotten tree; of which it is said, that it is to be cut down and cast into the fire (Matt. iii. 10; vii. 19). This root is not removed and a new one implanted in its stead, unless man regards evils which constitute the root as hurtful to his soul, and wills for that reason to put them away. But as they are of his *proprium*, and thence delightful, this is impossible except against his will and with struggling, thus with combat.

94. Every one who believes that there is a hell and a heaven, and that heaven is eternal happiness, and hell eternal misery; and who believes that those who do evil go to hell, and those that do good, to heaven, is brought into combat. And he who combats acts from an interior principle, and in opposition to the very concupiscence which constitutes the root of evil; for he who fights against anything does not will it, and to exercise concupiscence is to will. Hence it is evident, that the root of evil can only be removed by combat.

95. So far, therefore, as any one fights against and thus removes evil, so far good succeeds in its place; and so far from good he looks evil in the face, and then sees that it is infernal and horrible; and because it is so he not only shuns it, but even holds it in aversion, and at length abominates it.

96. The man who fights against evils cannot but fight as if from himself; for he who fights not as if from himself does not fight, but stands like an automaton, seeing nothing and doing nothing; and from evil he thinks continually in favor of evil, and not against it. But still it should be well known, that the Lord alone fights in man against evils, and that it only appears to man as if he fought from himself; and that the Lord wills that it should so appear to man, since without this appearance there could be no combat, and thus no reformation.

97. This combat is not grievous, except with those who have unloosed every restraint upon their concupiscences, and have intentionally indulged them; and also with those who have obstinately rejected the holy things of the Word and of the church. To others it is not grievous; let them resist evils in intention only once in a week, or twice in a month, and they will perceive a change.

98. The Christian church is called the church militant; and it cannot be termed militant except against the devil, thus against evils, which are from hell. The devil is hell. Temptation, which the man of the church undergoes, is this combat.

99. Combats against evils, which are temptations, are treated of in many places in the Word. They are meant by these

words of the Lord: "*Verily, I say unto you, Except a corn of wheat fall into the ground and die, it abideth alone, but if it die it bringeth forth much fruit*" (John xii. 24); and by these : "*Whosoever will come after me, let him renounce himself, and take up his cross, and follow me. Whosoever will save his life shall lose it; but whosoever shall lose his life for my sake and the gospel's, the same shall save it*" (Mark viii. 34, 35). By the cross is meant temptation; as also in Matt. x. 38; xvi. 24; Mark x. 21; Luke xiv. 27. By life is meant the life of man's *proprium*; as also in Matt. x. 39; xvi. 25; Luke ix. 24; and especially John xii. 25 ;—which is also the life of the flesh, that profiteth nothing, in John vi. 63. Concerning combats against evils, and victories over them, the Lord speaks to all the churches in the Revelation. Thus, to the CHURCH IN EPHESUS : "*To him that overcometh will I give to eat of the tree of life, which is in the midst of the paradise of God*" (Rev. ii. 7). To the CHURCH IN SMYRNA : "*He that overcometh shall not be hurt of the second death*" (Rev. ii. 11). To the CHURCH IN PERGAMOS : "*To him that overcometh will I give to eat of the hidden manna ; and will give him a white stone, and on the stone a new name written, which no one knoweth, saving he that receiveth it*" (Rev. ii. 17). To the CHURCH IN THYATIRA : "*He that overcometh, and keepeth my works unto the end, to him will I give power over the nations, and I will give him the morning star*" (Rev. ii. 26, 28). To the CHURCH IN SARDIS : "*He that overcometh, the same shall be clothed in white raiment*" (Rev. iii. 5). To the CHURCH IN PHILADELPHIA : "*Him that overcometh will I make a pillar in the temple of my God,—and I will write upon him the name of God, and the name of the city of God, the New Jerusalem, which cometh down out of heaven from God, and my new name*" (Rev. iii. 12). To the CHURCH IN LAODICEA : "*To him that overcometh, will I grant to sit with me in my throne*" (Rev. iii. 21).

100. These combats, which are temptations, may be seen particularly treated of in the work, ON THE NEW JERUSALEM AND ITS HEAVENLY DOCTRINE, published in London in 1758, n. 187—201. Whence and what they are, may be seen in n. 196, 197. How and when they occur, n. 198. What good they effect, n. 199. That the Lord fights for man, n. 200. Concerning the Lord's combats, or temptations, n. 201.

XIII. THAT MAN OUGHT TO SHUN EVILS AS SINS, AND TO FIGHT AGAINST THEM, AS IF FROM HIMSELF.

101. It is of divine order that man should act from freedom according to reason ; because to act from freedom according to reason is to act from himself. Yet in truth these two faculties, FREEDOM AND REASON, are not of man's *proprium*, but are of

the Lord with him. And in so far as he is a man they are not taken away from him, because without them he could not be reformed; for he could not do the work of repentance, he could not fight against evils, and afterwards bring forth fruits worthy of repentance. Now since freedom and reason are from the Lord with man, and man acts from them, it follows, that he does not act from himself, but as if from himself.*

102. The Lord loves man, and wills to dwell with him; yet He cannot love him and dwell with him unless He is received and loved reciprocally. Thence, and not otherwise, there is conjunction. For this cause the Lord has given to man freedom and reason; freedom to think and will as if from himself, and reason according to which [he may think and will]. To love and be conjoined with any one with whom there is no reciprocation is impossible; nor is it possible to enter into and remain with any one with whom there is no reception. Since the ability to receive and reciprocate are from the Lord in man, therefore the Lord says, " *Abide in me, and I in you* " (John xv. 4). " *He that abideth in me, and I in him, the same bringeth forth much fruit* " (John xv. 5). " *At that day ye shall know that—ye are in me, and I in you* " (John xiv. 20). That the Lord is in the truths and in the goods which man receives, and which are in him, He also teaches : " *If ye abide in me, and my words abide in you.—If ye keep my commandments, ye shall abide in my love* " (John xv. 7, 10). " *He that hath my commandments, and doeth them, he it is that loveth me,—and I will love him,—and will make my abode with him* " (John xiv. 21, 23). Thus the Lord dwells in his own with man; and man abides in those things which are from the Lord, and thus in the Lord.

103. Since man has from the Lord this power to reciprocate, or withhold reciprocation and thence mutual [love], therefore the Lord admonishes that man should repent;—and no one can repent, except as if from himself: " *Jesus said, Except ye repent, ye shall all perish* " (Luke xiii. 3, 5). *Jesus said, The kingdom of God is at hand; repent ye, and believe the Gospel* (Mark i. 15). *Jesus said, I come—to call sinners to repentance* (Luke v. 32). " *Jesus said to the churches, Repent* " (Rev. ii. 5, 16, 21, 22 ; iii. 3). Again, " *They repented not of their deeds* " (Rev. xvi. 11).

104. Because man has from the Lord this power to reciprocate or withhold reciprocation, and thence mutual [love], therefore the Lord enjoins, that man should do the commandments, and should bring forth fruits : " *Why call ye me Lord, Lord, and do not the things which I say ?* " (Luke vi. 46—49).

---

* That man has freedom from the Lord, may be seen above, n. 19, 20; and in the work on HEAVEN AND HELL, n. 589—596, 597—603. What freedom is, may be seen in the NEW JERUSALEM AND ITS HEAVENLY DOCTRINE, n. 141—149.

" If ye know these things, happy are ye if ye do them " (John
xiii. 17). *" Ye are my friends, if ye do whatsoever I command
you "* (John xv. 14). *" Whosoever shall do and teach, the same
shall be called great in the kingdom of the heavens "* (Matt. v.
19). *" Whosoever heareth my words, and doeth them, I will
liken him unto a prudent man "* (Matt. vii. 24). *" Bring forth
fruits worthy of repentance "* (Matt. iii. 8). *" Make the tree
good, and its fruit good "* (Matt. xii. 33). *" The kingdom shall
be—given to a nation bringing forth the fruits thereof "* (Matt.
xxi. 43). *" Every tree that bringeth not forth good fruit, is
hewn down and cast into the fire "* (Matt. vii. 19). And many
times in other places. From these passages it is evident, that
man acts from himself, but by the power of the Lord, which he
should implore; and this is to act as if from himself.

105. Because man has from the Lord this power to reciprocate or withhold reciprocation, and thence mutual [love],
therefore man will render an account of his works, and be
recompensed according to them ; for the Lord says, *" The Son
of Man shall come,—and render to every one according to his
works "* (Matt. xvi. 27). *" They that have done good shall come
forth to the resurrection of life, and they that have done evil to
the resurrection of judgment "* (John v. 29). *" Their works do
follow with them "* (Rev. xiv. 13). *All were judged according to
their works* (Rev. xx. 13). *" Behold I come, and my reward is
with me, to give to every one according as his work shall be "*
(Rev. xxii. 12). If there were with man no power of reciprocation there could be no imputation.

106. Because man has the ability to receive and reciprocate,
therefore the church teaches, that man should examine himself,
confess his sins before God, desist from them, and lead a new
life. That every church in the Christian world teaches this,
may be seen above (n. 3—8).

107. If there were not reception on the part of man, and
then thought as if from himself, nothing could have been said
about faith; for faith is not from man. Man would otherwise
be as chaff in the wind, and would stand as if inanimate, with
mouth open and hands down waiting for influx,—thinking
nothing, and doing nothing in those things which concern his
salvation. He indeed does nothing in those things [from him-
self], but yet he reacts as if from himself.

But these subjects will be placed in a still clearer light, in
the Treatises concerning ANGELIC WISDOM.

XIV. THAT IF ANY ONE SHUNS EVILS FOR ANY OTHER REASON
THAN BECAUSE THEY ARE SINS, HE DOES NOT SHUN THEM,
BUT ONLY PREVENTS THEIR APPEARING BEFORE THE EYES
OF THE WORLD.

108. THERE are moral men who keep the commandments of
the second table of the decalogue, who do not defraud, blaspheme,
revenge, or commit adultery; and those of them who confirm
themselves in the belief that such things are evil, because they
are hurtful to the common good, and so are contrary to the laws
of humanity, also live in the exercise of charity, sincerity,
justice, and chastity. But if they do these goods and shun
those evils only because they are evils, and not at the same time
because they are sins, they are still merely natural men; and
with those who are merely natural the root of evil remains
ingrafted, and is not removed. Therefore the good deeds which
they perform are not good, because they are from themselves.

109. A natural moral man may appear before the eyes of
men in the world altogether like a spiritual moral man; but not
before the angels in heaven. Before the angels in heaven, if he
be in good he appears as a statue of wood, and if in truths as
a statue of marble, in which there is no life. It is otherwise
with the spiritual moral man. For the natural moral man is
externally moral, and the spiritual moral man is internally
moral; and the external without the internal is not alive. It
lives indeed, but not the life which is called life.

110. The concupiscences of evil, which form the interiors of
man from his birth, are not removed except by the Lord alone.
For the Lord flows in from the spiritual into the natural; but
man of himself from the natural into the spiritual,—and this
influx is contrary to order, and does not operate upon concupiscences and remove them, but shuts them in more and more
closely in proportion as evil confirms itself. And as hereditary
evil thus shut in lies concealed, after death, when man becomes
a spirit, it bursts the covering in which it was hidden in the
world, and breaks forth as a corrupt discharge from an ulcer
that is but externally healed.

111. There are many and various causes which make man
moral in the external form; but if he be not also moral in the
internal form he is still not moral. For example:—If any
one abstain from adulteries and fornications through fear of the
civil law and its penalties; through fear of the loss of reputation, and thence of honor; through fear of diseases which may
be thereby contracted; through fear of family broils, from his
wife, and consequent intranquillity of life; through fear of
revenge, from the husband or his connections; through poverty
or avarice; through imbecility, arising either from disease, or
abuse, or from age, or from impotence; yea, if he abstain from
45

these evils on account of any natural or moral law, and not at the same time from a spiritual law, he is still inwardly an adulterer and fornicator; for he none the less believes that they are not sins, and hence does not in his spirit regard them as unlawful before God. And thus in spirit he commits them, although not before the world in the body; wherefore after death, when he becomes a spirit, he openly speaks in favor of them. It is evident from these considerations, that a wicked man may shun evils as hurtful; and that none but a Christian can shun evils as sins.

112. The case is the same in respect to thefts and frauds of every kind; in respect to murder and revenge of every kind; and every kind of false witness and lies. No one can be cleansed and purified from these of himself; for in each of these evils there are numberless concupiscences, which man does not see except as a single one, but the Lord sees the very least particulars in every series. In a word, man cannot regenerate himself,—that is, form in himself a new heart and a new spirit,—but the Lord alone, who is Himself the Reformer and Regenerator. If, therefore, from his own prudence and intelligence man wills to make himself anew, it is only like putting paint on a deformed face, and applying a cleansing medicine to a part affected with inward rottenness.

113. Therefore the Lord says in Matthew, "*Thou blind Pharisee, cleanse first the inside of the cup and the platter, that the outside of them may be clean also*" (xxiii. 26). And in Isaiah; "*Wash you, make you clean, put away the evil of your doings* FROM BEFORE MINE EYES, *cease to do evil;—and then though your sins be as scarlet, they shall be white as snow; though they be red like crimson, they shall be as wool*" (i. 16, 18).

114. To what has been said above let these words be added: I. That Christian charity, with every one, consists in his doing faithfully the duties of his calling; for thus, if he shuns evils as sins, he daily does good, and is himself his own particular use in the common body. Thus also the common good is provided for, and that of each individual in particular. II. That other works are not properly works of charity, but are either its signs, or benefits, or debts.

FINIS.

INDEX

TO THE

DOCTRINE OF LIFE

FOR THE

NEW JERUSALEM.

ACKNOWLEDGMENT of truth is faith in its genuine sense, 36.

ACT (To) from freedom according to reason, is to act from oneself, 101. But since freedom and reason are with man from the Lord, he does not act from himself, but as from himself, 101. Man has no active power in those things which concern his salvation, but still he has a power of reacting as from himself, 107.

ADULTERY. In a natural sense, by committing adultery, is also understood to act obscenely, to discourse lasciviously, and to think filthily; but in a spiritual sense, is meant to adulterate the goods of the Word, and to falsify its truths; and in a supreme sense, by committing adultery is meant to deny the Lord's divinity and to profane the Word, 74. Adultery is so great an evil that it may be called essentially diabolical, 74. Whosoever is principled in natural adultery, is also in spiritual adultery, and vice versâ, 74. So far as any one shuns adulteries of every kind as sins, so far he loves chastity, 74—79. By committing adultery in a spiritual sense, is meant to adulterate the good of the Word, 74, ill. 79.

ANGEL (An) is an angel from the love and wisdom which he has, 32. There are angels who receive more of divine good than of divine truth, and there are others who receive more of divine truth than of divine good, 32. Still the angels of all the heavens are so far in wisdom and intelligence, as good with them makes a one with truth, 32.

1

ARK (The). Why the ark was called "Jehovah-There," 55, ill. 59.

ARTIFICER. Illustration of the love of good for truth, by application to the case of an artificer, 39.

AS FROM HIMSELF. Man ought to do good from himself, but by the Lord's power, which he should implore, and this is to do good as from himself, 104.

ASSYRIA signifies reasoning, 79.

ATHANASIAN CREED (Doctrine of the) in regard to the Trinity, 3.

AUTOMATON. If man does not combat as from himself against evils, he is like an automaton, 96.

AVERSION. It is not possible for any one to shun evils as sins, so as to hold them inwardly in aversion, except by combats against them, 92—100.

BABYLON signifies the profanation of good, 79. By Babylon are meant those who arrogate to themselves the divine power of the Lord, and profane the Word by adulterating and falsifying it, 79.

Obs. Babylon signifies the Roman Catholic religion, D. P. 264. It is the love of ruling over the holy things of the Church from self-love, A. R. 717.

BEAST. The ground of distinction between man and beast, 15.

BELIEVE (To) in the Lord is not only to think that He is, but also to do His words, as he elsewhere teaches, 48.

BENEFITS of charity, 114.

BIRTH. Evils inwardly concealed in man from birth, 68, 69.

BLASPHEME. By bearing false witness, is meant in the supreme sense, to blaspheme the Lord and the Word, 87.

BORN (The) of the will of the flesh, and of the will of man, are such as will and act, and think and speak, from their *proprium*, 17. Those who are born of God are such as will and act, and think and speak from the Lord, 17.

BREAD signifies good, 40. Comparison of bread and wine, in regard to the love of good for truth, 40.

CAUSE (The) is called the mediate end, 14.

CHALDEA signifies the profanation of truth, 79.

CHARIOT (A) denotes doctrine from the understanding, 30.

CHARITY (Christian) consists in a man's performing faithfully the duties of his calling, 114.

CHASTITY. So far as any one shuns adulteries of every kind as sins, so far he loves chastity, 74—79. The chastity of marriage and the lasciviousness of adultery are two opposites, 75. The chastity of marriage abides only with those who shun the lasciviousness of adultery as sin, 76. It is impossible for any one to know what the chastity of marriage is, unless he shuns the lasciviousness of adultery as sin, 76. The chastity of marriage makes heaven with man, 76.

CHRISTIAN. How it may be concluded whether a man be a Christian or not, 77. None but a Christian can shun evils as sins; a wicked person may shun them as being hurtful, 111.

CHURCH. Why the Christian Church is called the Church militant, 98.

CITIZEN. By civil good, and according to it, man is a citizen in the natural world, but by spiritual good, and according to it, he is a citizen in the spiritual world, 12. See *Good.*

CIVIL. The man who is principled in spiritual good, is a moral man, and also a civil man, whereas the man who is not principled in spiritual good, appears as if he were a moral and civil man, but still he is not so in reality, 13, 14. Civil good, with a man who is principled in spiritual good, is ultimate spiritual good, 14. See *Good.* Civil conduct serves to cover the evils concealed inwardly with man from his birth, 68.

CLOUD. The concupiscences of evil are as a black cloud beneath the spiritual mind, 86.

COMBAT (To). Man ought to combat against evils as from himself, 100—

107. He who combats, acts from an interior principle, and in opposition to that concupiscence which constitutes the root of the evil, 94. The man who fights against evils, must needs combat as from himself; otherwise he does not fight, 96. Still the Lord alone fights in man against evils, and it only appears to man as if he fought from himself, 96.

COMBATS against evils are temptations, 99; such combat is not grievous, except to those who have given up the reins to their concupiscences, and also to those who have confirmed themselves in the rejection of the holy things of the Word and of the church, 97.

COMPARISON of man to a garden during winter, and during summer, 86. Comparison between a living faith and a dead faith, 46. Comparison between good deeds done from God and from man's self, 10. Comparison in regard to the cases of a priest, a soldier, a merchant, and an artificer, 39; in regard to meat and water, bread, and wine, 40; with a tree, 46.

CONCUPISCENCE (To have) is to will, 94. The concupiscences of evil which form the interiors of man from his birth, are not removed except by the Lord alone, 110. Why man of himself does not operate upon concupiscences to the removal of them, but encloses them more and more closely, 110. The concupiscences of evil close up the interiors of the natural mind on the part of the will, 86. There are infinite concupiscences inherent in every evil, 112. Concupiscence constitutes the root of evil, 94. All concupiscence remains with man after death, 63.

CONJUNCTION of heaven with man, 3. Conjunction of good with truth, 32. The conjunction of good and truth is called the celestial marriage, and the conjunction of evil and falsity is called the infernal marriage, 33. The conjunction of faith and life is effected like the conjunction of truth and of good, each resembling the conjunction of the understanding and the will, 44. The conjunction of the will and the understanding with man is meant in the Word by the heart and soul, and by the heart and spirit, 86. The conjunction of the Lord with man, and of man with the Lord, is effected by the law of the Ten Commandments, 57.

CONSOCIATION. Covenants made for the sake of consociation, 60.

2

Obs. The word *consociation* is used to give the exact meaning of the Latin word, *consociatio*; the word *association* is not suitable, there being a sensible difference between *consociation* and *association.*

COVENANT (A) signifies conjunction, 57, *ill.* 60.

CROSS (By the) is understood temptation, 99. To take up the cross, Mark x. 21, signifies to fight against concupiscences, 66.

CUNNING insinuates itself even into the spiritual mind of man, 81, 85.

DEBTS of charity, 114.

DECALOGUE (The) teaches what evils are sins, 53—61. The laws of the Decalogue were the first fruits of the Word, 54; they contained a brief summary of all things relating to religion, whereby the conjunction of the Lord with man, and of man with the Lord, is effected, 54. Why these laws, so universally known throughout the earth, should be promulgated in so miraculous a manner, 53. Why the law of the Decalogue is called the Covenant and the Testimony, 57.

DECEIT insinuates itself even into the spiritual mind of man, 81, 85.

DEFAME (To). By bearing false witness, is also meant to defame, 87.

DENY (To). By committing adultery, in the supreme sense, is meant to deny the Lord's divinity, 74.

DEVIL. Hell is the devil, 98. Unless man were reformed, he would become a devil, 68.

DISTINCTION between man and beast, 15.

DIVINE. The divine good and divine truth are the two universals which proceed from the Lord, 32. Divine good is of His divine love, and divine truth is of His divine wisdom, 32. Those two in the Lord are a one, and thence proceed as a one from Him, 32.

Do (To) has relation to the will, and to think has relation to the understanding, 42. In the Word, by doing the truth is meant the causing good to exist, 39. No one can do good from himself, 9 and following, 31. Man ought to do good from himself, but by the Lord's power, which he should implore, 104.

DWELL (To). The Lord loves man and wills to dwell with him, 102. The Lord dwells in His own with man, and man in those things which are from the Lord, and thus in the Lord, 102.

3

EFFECT (The) is called the ultimate end, 14. See *End.*

EGYPT, denotes science, 30, 79.

END (The), cause and effect, make one; the end itself is called the primary end, the cause the mediate end, and the effect the ultimate end, 14.

ENGLAND. Exhortation which is publicly read in England previous to the celebration of the Lord's Supper, 4.

ENMITIES. By murders are understood also enmities, 67.

EQUILIBRIUM between heaven and hell, man is in this equilibrium, 20 (note).

ESSE AND EXISTERE (The). Good is the very *esse* of a thing, and truth is the *existere* of a thing thence derived, 43. The will, with man, is the very *esse* of his life, and the understanding is the *existere* of his life thence derived, 43. The thought of the understanding derives its *existere* from the love of the will, which is the *esse* of the thought in the understanding, 48.

ESSENCE (The) of good cannot possibly originate in any other but in Him who is good itself, 13.

EVIL is hell, 18. Evil loves falsity, and falsity loves evil, and they are desirous of being a one, 33. Evils which ought to be shunned as sins, 62—66. So far as man shuns evils as sins, so far he does what is good, not from himself, but from the Lord, 18—31. Evils prevent the Lord's entrance into man, 18. Man commits evils from delight, if destitute of religion, 92.

EXERCISES (Religious) which are the effect of habit only, or meritorious, or hypocritical, 25, 26.

EXHORTATION publicly read in England previous to the celebration of the Sacrament of the Lord's Supper, 5, 6.

EXISTERE. See *Esse.*

EXTERNAL (What is) without what is internal is not alive; it lives indeed, but not the life which is called *life*, 109. Man lays aside his external with the body when he dies, and retains the internal, 68.

FACULTIES. Man has two faculties, one of which is called the will and the other the understanding, 43. They are distinct from each other, but are so created that they may become a one, 43. They constitute the human mind, and all the life of man therein, 43. These two faculties are the receptacles and subjects of good and truth, 43. They form one mind as good and truth make a one, 43.

FAITH. The acknowledgment of truth is faith in its genuine sense, 36. It is the office of faith to know and to think, and still more to understand that a thing is so, 44. Faith is of truth, and truth is of faith, 43. Faith and life are distinct from each other, like thinking and doing, 42; likewise the will and understanding, 42. Man is not endowed with a grain of faith, except so far as it is conjoined with life, 52. Faith and life march on with equal step, 52. The conjunction of faith and of life, is like the conjunction of truth and of good, 44. Faith, with those who are spiritual, is truth, 50. So far as any one shuns evils as sins, so far he has faith, and is a spiritual man, 42—52. Man may believe he has faith, and yet have it not, if he is in evil of life, 44. The evil of life and the truth of faith, can never act as a one, 44. The evil of life destroys the truth of faith, 44. The faith of a wicked man is intellectual faith, in which there is no good from the will, consequently, it is a dead faith, 46. Truths which appear to belong to faith only, 47; these truths of faith are dead with the man who is principled in evil, but alive with him who is in good, 47. They who are in evils have no faith, however they may suppose that they have, 49.

FALSIFY (To). By committing adultery, is understood in the spiritual sense, to falsify the truths of the Word, 74, 79.

FILTHILY. By committing adultery is meant also to think filthily, 74.

FIRST-FRUITS of the Word and of the Israelitish Church, 54.

FLESH signifies man's proprium, 30.

FLOW-IN (To). The Lord flows-in with man from what is spiritual into what is natural, whereas man of himself enters from what is natural into what is spiritual, 110.

FOOLISH ONE. He who supposes that salvation consists in believing this or that doctrine which the Church teaches, and is still an evil doer, must needs be called a foolish one, 91.

FORMATION of good, 37.

FRAUD and sincerity are two opposites, wherefore so far as any one is not in fraud, so far he is in sincerity, 82.

FREEDOM and reason are not of man's proprium, but are of the Lord within him, 101. Man should act from freedom according to reason, 101. The Lord has given to man freedom to think and will as from himself, 102. Without freedom man could not be re-

formed, 101. Man during his abode in the world, is kept in the liberty of turning himself either to evil or good, and this freedom is never taken away from any one, 19, 20. Every man has this freedom, not from himself but from the Lord, 20.

FRUIT (John xv. 5), signifies good, 17.

FULFIL (To). A religious persuasion has prevailed that no one can fulfil the law, 63. Disastrous result of this declaration, 63.

GOD is good itself, 13. That good not from God, but from man, is not good, 13.

GOLD. Comparison of good deeds with gold, 10.

GOOD (All) comes from the Lord, 17. The good which proceeds not from God, but from man, is not good, 13. Good relates to charity, 9. Good which is of the will, forms itself in the understanding, and in a certain manner, renders itself visible, 43. There is civil good, moral good, and spiritual good, 12. Civil good is that which man does whilst acting under the influence of the law of the land. Moral good is that which man does whilst acting under the influence of the law of reason. Spiritual good is what a man does whilst acting under the influence of a spiritual law, 12. Spiritual good has the essence of good in it, 13. Consequently, it includes moral and civil good also, 13. Spiritual good is the supreme, moral good is the middle, and civil good is the ultimate, 12. Doing good and thinking good form a one, 1. To do good two things are required; first, that a man ought to shun evils because they are sins ; and second, to shun them as from himself, but to know and believe that he does so from the Lord, 22. No one can be in good and at the same time in evil, 28. No one can do good which is really good from himself, 9—17 ; but he can do it from the Lord, 29. So far as man is not purified from evils, his good deeds are not good, 30. If a man wills and does what is good, before he shuns evils as sins, the good things which he wills and does are not good, 23, 24. The reason why, 24. Good is not good unless it be conjoined with truth, 37. Concerning good in the case of a priest, a merchant, or an artificer, 39, 72 ; of a soldier, 39 ; of a magistrate, 72.

Obs. In the writings of our Author, when good only is treated of, spiritual good is always meant; if any other kind of good is intended, it is called natural, moral, or civil good.

Good and Truth. Good is the very *esse* of a thing, and truth is the *existere* of a thing thence derived, 43. Good and truth are a one in the Lord, and proceed as a one from Him, 32, 33. Good loves truth, and truth loves good, and they desire to be a one, 33, 39. The conjunction of good and truth is called the celestial marriage, 33. Good conjoined with truth constitutes love and wisdom with an angel and with man, 32. Good relates to the will, truth to the understanding, 36. From the love of good in the will, proceeds the love of truth in the understanding, 36.

Habit. Religious exercises which are the effect of habit only, 25.

Harlot (A) corresponds to the falsification of truth, and thence signifies it, 46.

Hatred. By murders are understood also hatreds, 67.

Heart (The) signifies the will, 51. By the heart is meant the will and its love, 86.

Heat (Spiritual) is the divine love, 86. The heat of heaven is love, 15.

Heavens (The) are distinguished into two kingdoms; one of which is called the celestial kingdom, the other the spiritual kingdom, 32. The heavens which receive more of the divine good constitute the celestial kingdom, but those which receive more of the divine truth constitute the spiritual kingdom, 32. The Lord is heaven, 18. The chastity of marriage makes heaven with man, 76.

Hell is the devil, 98. Evil is hell, 18. The lasciviousness of adultery makes hell with man, 76.

Hereditary evil, concealed by man, bursts its covering after death, and breaks out, like the discharge from an ulcer which had been only superficially healed, 110.

Horse (A) signifies the understanding, 30. The horses of the Egyptians signify man's own intelligence, 30.

Horseman (A) signifies intelligence from doctrine, 30.

Hypocritical. Exercises of piety which are hypocritical, 25, 26.

Influx (The) with man, from what is spiritual into what is natural, is contrary to order, and does not operate upon concupiscences to the removal of them, but encloses them more and more closely in proportion as it confirms itself, 110.

Ingrafted. With men merely natural, the root of evil remains ingrafted, and is not removed, 108.

Intelligence (Of the) which proceeds from man, and of that which comes from the Lord, 30.

Internal (The) is what produces, 72. See *External*.

Jehovah. Why the ark was called "Jehovah-There," 55. Shewn, 59.

Jerusalem signifies the Church, 79.

Kingdom. The heavens are distinguished into two kingdoms; one of which is called the celestial kingdom, the other the spiritual kingdom, 32. The heavens which receive more of the divine good than of divine truth, constitute the celestial kingdom, 32. Those which receive more of the divine truth, constitute the spiritual kingdom, 32.

Know (To). Man may know that in which he is, but he cannot know that in which he is not, 76. To know anything in which he is not by description, or by thinking about it, is not to know it, 76.

Knowledges appertaining to the understanding only, and not to the will, are without life, and perish in time, 27; after death, the man himself casts them off, 27. Still, however, knowledges are highly necessary, because they teach how a man ought to act, 27.

Lasciviously. By committing adultery is understood also to discourse lasciviously, 74. The lasciviousness of adultery and the chastity of marriage are two opposites; wherefore so far as man is not in the one, so far he is in the other, 75. The lasciviousness of adultery makes hell with man, 76.

Laws (The) of the Decalogue contained a brief summary of all things relating to religion, whereby the conjunction of the Lord with man, and of man with the Lord, is effected, 54. They were the first-fruits of the Word, 54; and were most holy, 55. Why those laws were promulgated from Mount Sinai, by Jehovah Himself, in so miraculous a manner, though so universally known throughout the earth, 53.

Lie. So far as any one shuns a lie as sin, so far he loves truth, 88.

Lie (To). By bearing false witness, is also understood, in a natural sense, to lie, 87.

LIFE (The) of man is his love, 1. The life of religion is to do good, 1, 8. The life after death remains such as it was in the world, 8. An evil life cannot after death be changed into a good life, nor a good life into an evil life, 8. A good life is called life, and an evil life is called death, 8.

LIGHT (Spiritual) is the divine wisdom, 86. The light of heaven is truth, 15.

LIVE (To). Whosoever lives well will be saved, and whosoever lives wickedly will be condemned, 1; 3.

LORD (The) is Good itself, and Truth itself, 38. There are two universals which proceed from the Lord, divine good and divine truth, 32. The Lord is with man, in good and in truth, 38. *Shewn*, 102. The Lord dwells in His own with man, 102. If the truth is loved from good, then the Lord is loved, *shewn*, 38. To follow the Lord, Mark x. 21, signifies to acknowledge the Lord to be God, 66.

Obs. By the Lord, in the writings of the Author, Jesus Christ, the Saviour of the world, is alone signified, *A. C.* 14.

LOVE is of good, and good is of love, 43. Good conjoined with truth constitutes love and wisdom with an angel and with man, 32. So far as any one shuns murders of every kind as sins, so far he has love towards his neighbour, 67—72.

LOVE (To). What a man loves he not only does willingly, but also thinks willingly, 1. Whatsoever any one wills from love, that he wills to do, to think, to understand, and to speak, 48. Good loves truth, and truth loves good, and they desire to be a one; likewise evil loves falsity, and falsity loves evil, and they are desirous of being a one, 33.

LUKEWARM. If two opposites were together, there would result that lukewarm state spoken of, Rev. iii. 16, 71.

MAGISTRATE, who is in the good of love towards his neighbour, 72. Whatsoever he does is a good work, 72.

MAN (A) is distinguished from an animal by this, that he has a spiritual mind, whereby he has a capacity of being in heaven during his abode in the world, 86. So long as the concupiscences of evils close up the interiors of the natural mind, so long man is an animal, 86; differing only in this, that he can think and speak, even concerning such things as he does not see with his eyes, 86. Man is man from the

love and wisdom which he has, 32. Man becomes truly a man, when he thinks what is true in the understanding, from good in the will, 86. Man, during his abode in the world, is in the midst between hell and heaven, or between the Lord and the devil; or, what is the same thing, between evil and good, 19, 69. Man ought to shun evils as sins, and to combat against them as from himself, 101—107. So far as man shuns evils as sins, so far he does what is good not from himself, but from the Lord, 18. Man is so constituted that he is enabled to shun evils as of himself by power derived from the Lord, if he implore it, 31. The man who is principled in spiritual good is a moral man and also a civil man, 13. The man who is not principled in spiritual good, is neither a moral nor a civil man, 14. See *Good*. They are called natural men, with whom what is moral and civil is natural as to its essence; but they are called spiritual men, with whom what is moral and civil is spiritual as to its essence, 16. Natural men do good from themselves, but spiritual men do good from the Lord, 16. Man after death is such as his life has been in the world, 8.

MARRIAGE. The conjunction of good and truth is called the celestial marriage, and the conjunction of evil and falsity the infernal marriage, 33. In the heavenly marriage heaven is, in which the Church will be, 42. A similar marriage exists between the will and the understanding, as between good and truth, 43.

MEANS of reformation provided by the Lord, 69.

MEAT or bread alone does not suffice for nourishment without water or wine, 40. By meat or bread, in the Word, is meant good, 40.

MERCHANT (A) who is in the good of love towards his neighbour, 72. Whatsoever he does is a good work, 72. Comparison of a merchant in regard to the love of good for truth, 39.

MERITORIOUS. Exercises of piety, which are meritorious, 25, 26.

MIDDLE. The supreme, the middle, and the end, make one, like end, cause, and effect, 14.

MIDST. Man, during his abode in the world, is in the midst between heaven and hell, or between the Lord and the devil, or between good and evil, 19, 69.

MIND. The will and understanding constitute the human mind and all the life of man therein, 43, 85. The will and understanding form one mind, as good and truth form a one, 43. Man has a natural mind and a spiritual mind, 81, 86. The natural mind is beneath, and the spiritual mind is above, 86. The natural mind may be called the *animal* mind, but the spiritual mind the *human* mind, 86. By his spiritual mind, man has a capacity of being in heaven, during his abode in the world; by this also it is that man lives after death, 86.

MORAL conduct, by which man learns to cover over the interior evils concealed within him from birth, 68.

MORAL good, in the case of the man who is principled in spiritual good, is middle spiritual good, 14. See *Good*. The man who is principled in spiritual good, is a moral man and also a civil man; whereas, the man who is not principled in spiritual good, appears as if he were a moral and civil man, but still he is not so in reality, 13, 14. Concerning a natural moral man, and a spiritual moral man, how both appear before the angels, 109. There are various and manifold causes operating to render man moral in an external form, 111; but if he is not also moral in an internal form, he is still not moral, 111.

MURDER. In the natural sense, by murders of every kind are understood also enmities, hatreds, and revenge of every kind; in a spiritual sense, are meant all modes of killing and destroying the souls of men; and in a supreme sense, is meant, to hate the Lord, 67. These three kinds of murder make a one, and cohere together, 67; they lie concealed inwardly with man from his birth, 68. So far as any one shuns murders of every kind as sins, so far he has love towards his neighbour, 67 —72. The evil of murder is opposite to the good of neighbourly love, 70.

NATURAL MEN. Those who do good from themselves are called natural men; but those who do good from the Lord are called spiritual men, 16.

NOURISHMENT. Good derives its nourishment and formation from truths, 37. Meat, or bread alone, does not suffice for nourishment, without water or wine, 40.

OBSCENELY. By committing adultery is also meant to act obscenely, 74.

OPERATIVE (An) who is in the good of love towards his neighbour, 72. All the deeds done by such are good works, 72.

OPPOSITE. Conversion into an opposite is extinction, 8. Two opposites cannot abide together, 71.

ORDER (Divine). It is of divine order that man should act from freedom according to reason, 101.

PARABLE concerning works, 2; parable of the sower explained, 90.

PERCEPTION. Whence is derived the general perception that there is a God, 3. Its effect in Christian Churches, 4. When general perception is given, 7. From the love of truth proceeds the perception of truth; from the perception of truth, the thought of truth, 36. Obs. Perception is a sensation proceeding only from the Lord, relating to good and truth, *A. C.* 104. Perception consists in seeing that truth is truth, and good is good, and in seeing that evil is evil, and that the false is false, *A. C.* 7680.

PERFECT. Men are perfect when the Lord is in them, 84.

PERISH. The things which perish in time, 27.

PIOUS (The) things which a man thinks and speaks before he shuns evils as sins, are not pious, 23. The reason why, 25. Shewn, 30.

POWER of the law in the ark, 56.

PRIEST (A) who is in the good of love towards his neighbour, 72. Whatsoever he does is a good work, 72. Comparison concerning a priest, on the love of good for truth, 39.

PRIESTHOOD. The good of the priesthood consists in providing for the salvation of souls, 39.

PROFANE (To). By committing adultery, in the supreme sense, is meant to profane the Word, 74.

PROGRESSION from the love of good to faith, 36.

PROMULGATION of the law, 53.

PROPRIUM (The) of man is evil from his birth, 92. This proprium constitutes the first root of man's life, 93.

RATIONAL. So long as the will is not with the understanding in heaven, man is not rational, though he may think and discourse rationally, 15.

REASON and freedom are not of man's proprium, but are of the Lord within him, 101. Man should act from freedom according to reason, 101. The Lord has given to man reason, according to which he may think and will freely as from himself, 102. Without reason man could not be reformed, 101.

7

and causes it to act as a one with itself, 44. In John i. 13, the will of the flesh is the proprium, or selfhood of man's will, which in itself is evil, and the will of man is the proprium of his understanding, which in itself is falsity derived from evil, 17.

WILL (To). Whatsoever any one wills from love, that he wills to do, to think, to understand, and to speak, 48.

WILL and Understanding. The will with man is the very *esse* of his life, and the understanding is the *existere* of his life, 43. All things with man have relation to the will and the understanding, 43. The will is the receptacle and subject of all things of good, and the understanding the receptacle and subject of all things of truth, 43. The will and understanding form one mind, as good and truth make a one, 43. A similar marriage exists between the will and understanding, as between good and truth, 43. Good which is of the will, forms itself in the understanding, and in a certain manner renders itself visible, 43. The understanding of man is capable of being elevated into the light of heaven which is truth, and of seeing by that light, but it is possible for the will of man not to be elevated in like manner into the heat of heaven, which is love, and not to act under its influ-

ence, 15. So long as the will is not with the understanding in heaven, man is not spiritual and consequently not rational, 15. The understanding does not lead the will, but the will the understanding, 15; the understanding only teaching and pointing out the way, 15. Thinking has relation to the understanding, and doing has relation to the will, 42.

WIND signifies truth, 40.

WISDOM. If a man knows and is wise about many things, and does not shun evils as sins, he has no wisdom, 23. The reason why, 27. *Shewn* 30.

WITNESS. By bearing false witness in a natural sense, is not only meant to act in the character of a false witness, but also to lie and to defame. By bearing false witness in a spiritual sense, is meant to assert, and to persuade others, that what is false is true, and that what is evil is good, and *vice versâ*, and in the supreme sense is meant to blaspheme the Lord and the Word, 87. So far as any one shuns false witness of every kind as sins, so far he loves truth, 87—91.

WORKS are what constitute man a member of the church, and he is saved according thereto, 2. All the works of man are either good or evil, according as there is interiorly within him either good or evil, 72. Examples, 72.

10

www.ingramcontent.com/pod-product-compliance
Lightning Source LLC
Chambersburg PA
CBHW031758090426
42739CB00008B/1066